# VERMONT COLLEGE
## MONTPELIER, VERMONT

Florence Rempel

# THE CIRCLING YEAR

*Books by*

*Frederic F. Van de Water*

•

RUDYARD KIPLING'S VERMONT FEUD
A HOME IN THE COUNTRY
WE'RE STILL IN THE COUNTRY
FATHERS ARE FUNNY
THE CIRCLING YEAR
THE FAMILY FLIVVERS TO FRISCO
ELMER 'N' EDWINA
STILL WATERS
PLUNDER
THE REAL MC COY
THUNDER SHIELD
GLORY HUNTER: A LIFE OF GENERAL CUSTER
HIDDEN WAYS

The first five titles listed above are published by
The John Day Company

# THE
# CIRCLING YEAR

Frederic F. Van de Water

*NEW YORK*

THE JOHN DAY COMPANY

# CONTENTS

# THE CIRCLING YEAR

# CHAPTER ONE

# January

THIS IS the time when Althea and I know that the new, year-long voyage begins. Deepening snow and waxing cold, the bitter glare of days and the nights' arctic silences, earlier dawns and the perceptible seconds added to each pale sunset make us aware that Earth stands out to sea once more.

She heels as sail is made. We watch, while her rail goes down, how the sun stands each day a small space higher in the sky. His strengthening light armors the drifts and magnifies icicles along the eaves. We have cast off. Our packet is outward bound again, traveling the great circle from Capricorn to Aquarius, Pisces, Aries and all the twelve ports of the zodiac, and Althea and I are humble and temporary sharcholders in her immemorial venture.

This, too, is the time when our city-dwelling kin and friends most pity us.

Once, they sighed over our abysmal ignorance and our plan to spend a winter in Vermont. They predicted, among themselves, that we never should be able to endure the loneliness, the cold privations and perils that all New Yorkers are sure maintain in January north of the

Bronx. We didn't, they told each other and us, know what we were doing. One winter, or a fraction thereof, would cure us.

And now we are deep in our sixth winter here. Our friends have become less charitable. It can't be ignorance any longer. It must be insanity.

Two normal folk who have known Manhattan's heady delights would not foreswear them for a remodeled farmhouse on drift-swamped hillside acres nine miles from even a moving picture. No mentally sound couple could find in such frigid isolation compensation for the music and the plays, the restaurants and the revelry, the color and the glitter of New York.

Did we, our friends asked us with the gentle patronage reserved for the mentally afflicted, really find our bleak property more alluring than Times Square? Was companionship with each other and several obviously unintellectual dogs, with possibly now and then a call from a seal or an Eskimo, all the society we thought we needed?

By our answer they proclaimed us not only demented but incurable. Our urban friends and relatives told each other baldly and us more tactfully how much they pitied us. Out of our self-imposed plight, they derived the peculiarly sustaining comfort that comes from considering the wretchedness of others.

Folk in an East Side flat, recalling our household, our surroundings, our way of life, and matching these against their own, are cheered and fortified. None of them ever has confessed it, yet I am sure it must be so, because I do know that Althea and I, through Vermont's Januaries, add additional savor to life by thinking with an equally unsought sympathy of the unfortunates who live in New York.

Our condescension is reprehensible yet natural. It is the instinctive superiority folk in the first cabin display toward passengers in the steerage. City dwellers are embedded in man-made surroundings. The excitement and the spectacle of the annual voyage are not for them. Only an occasional glimpse through a porthole assures them that they are moving at all. Althea and I, by grace of our partnership with a Vermont farm, have chairs on the sun deck with the world's spacious beauties all about us.

We watch the curved wake of our journey spin out behind, and ahead we can see on the horizon the loom of beloved headlands soon to be revisited. We have the wind and the sun, the stars and the responsive loveliness of earth for our intimates, and if that sounds like something clumsily pilfered from George Borrow, Althea and I are sorry but it happens to be exactly the way we feel.

Five times now we have cruised through all the months of that circular passage. Now, as the sixth voyage begins, our hearts and hopes are higher than on any earlier sailing.

Scufflings in the antechamber to our bedroom, where our dogs slumber, woke me at sunrise this morning. I rose and, swathed in a woolen bathrobe, let Dougal and Meg, the Scottish terriers, and Black Boy, the Newfoundland, lead me with clamor down the stair.

I opened the front door. Black Boy cavorted out, Meg

followed demurely and Dougal plodded in the rear with an "Oh, my good God; more snow!" expression in his whiskered Calvinistic face.

The porch was covered with soft flakes into which he sank. The hillside shone in the queer light which is neither pink nor yellow that the new sun spreads, and long tree shadows were streaks of clear blue upon the drifts. The cold crawled in beneath my tight-drawn bathrobe. It tingled in my nose like an incautious gulp of champagne. No breath of wind moved across the frigid brilliance. Last night's snow lay undisturbed upon the locusts' pied branches so that two trees, a sturdier dark and a spindlier white, seemed now to grow in union where last night only one had stood.

The fall had cleansed our dooryard of stain or track. It had rounded the contours of the shoulder-high barricades the plow had piled on either side of the driveway and, in the wake of Black Boy's frenzied gambolings, small crystals blazed in the sunlight with the still fire of gems.

The terriers came back into the house, shaking off clotted snow. Black Boy was too enraptured to heed until I had called him twice. He wallowed in drifts. He gobbled vast mouthfuls. Before I summoned him a second time, I thought: I have seen all this—the snow and the tender shadows and the heart-catching early light—each of the five winters we have lived here and this sixth, repeating the theme once more, seems richer and fairer than all its forerunners. And the next and the next and the twentieth hence, if I endure so long, will be lovelier still. It is strange that this should be so.

A chickadee, one animate particle in the barren glare of morning, lit on the feeding tray and paused, before he kicked snow away and breakfasted, to jeer at Black Boy. I thought: Perhaps it isn't so very strange. All life's importances increase in value with repetition. Existence is sweet because, forever, one returns again. The beloved thing, whether it be flesh or stone, music or print or canvas; spring, summer, autumn or winter, grows dearer still with each reunion.

I found myself shivering and I called my Newfoundland sharply. Black Boy galloped back into the house. I closed the door but I stood and looked through its side panes at the morning's splendor.

Winter had completely repossessed our household. The circling year had brought us back to where we had been twelve months ago. January now saw our packet swing out into space again, through seas we had sailed, toward harbors we had visited five times since we came to live in the country, and another twelve months would bring us back to this very port.

Althea and I would find even greater happiness in this voyage than in its predecessors. Each month through which we journeyed might promise less of adventure and bewilderment than it had brought us in the past, but a sense of requital, of longing fulfilled and memories become actual again, would brighten every day of our passage.

Black Boy whined beside me and we turned and went upstairs together, he eager to wake Althea by thrusting a snowy muzzle into her unappreciative face, I still fumbling with thoughts that spread warmth inside me yet dodged imprisonment in words.

By coming here, by living for five years upon our own land, we had forsaken a city's importunate rhythms and had been increasingly possessed by the graver cadence of the year. We moved no more along the tangents of human insurgence. We had surrendered to the deliberate course of life itself, that travels a curve sooner or later closed.

I told the newly wakened Althea all this when she had justifiably slapped Black Boy. She listened to me with that dazed look my philosophizing brings to any face and, most often, to her own.

"The point is," I ended, "that life is a series of complete circuits. Each day, each year is a circle. The course of duty, or what man calls duty, may be a straight line, but all important matters progress in ovals and ellipses and return at last to the beginning. The daily movement of each of us is an erratic loop, away from home and back to it, out of bed and finally into bed again. Animate dust circles at last to dust once more, just as earth wheeling through space will bring another January morning like this to us when the complete circle has been drawn."

"His nose," said Althea, looking at Black Boy, "was very cold, but I didn't mean to slap him so hard."

"We," I said resolutely, "are more and more content here because we move in the way it was ordained that men should go. We're part of our own earth and subject to its laws and whims. And we're paid for our servitude in the sort of happiness city dwellers can't understand."

Althea leaned out of bed, looking for her slippers.

"Antaeus," I told her loudly, "wasn't just a myth. The Greeks were smart people. They had found out that contact with the soil gives one odd strength, an alliance with the things of earth itself that grows firmer with each new encounter. You and I are like Antaeus. We—"

"You mean," Althea asked, blinking, "that each year we have spent here has been sweeter because of the memories and knowledge and insight we have gained?"

"Something like that."

"Goodness," Althea said. "I found that out long ago —before we had been in Vermont two years. Life here is like listening to a Beethoven symphony. It grows lovelier and you find more in it every time you enjoy it."

She sought a warmer room to dress and was followed by a repentant Newfoundland. Black Boy's most endearing trait is his eagerness to apologize excessively for any pain, inadvertent or deliberate, inflicted upon him. Althea left me with that sense of dismay all husbands know. This is the empty feeling that comes when one finds his own brand-new discovery has been his wife's long-held property. Althea, too, had said more in her brief exit speech than all my windy verbiage had been able to accomplish.

We whose senses are tuned to the year's symphony find fresh grace and exaltation in the replaying of each of its four movements. The glee of adventure never entirely vanishes, but it wanes with repetition. A serener happiness, the calm joy of recognition, takes its place.

[ 9 ]

Here, on our Vermont farm, the music forever is in our ears—strong and clear when we stop to listen, unobtrusively present even when other matters occupy us.

I followed Althea's simile further while I dressed myself with the unscrupulous haste a January morning imposes. For the sixth time we had settled ourselves in our seats, close to the podium of the Conductor, to hear the grave and lovely opening measures. After five previous playings, we knew the score practically by heart. Neither inattention nor boredom would rise from this knowledge. Because we were aware where each new theme would intrude, we should listen more intently for its advent. We should anticipate and greet cherished passages. We should match the current rendition against the earlier. We should file the present playing away in our memories for other, future comparisons.

"This is the coldest January morning we have had since 1935." "We had just such a sunset as this in 1937. Remember?" "We're due for a thaw now; we always get one when the sky looks like this."

Such apparently meretricious, actually precious knowledge is compensation to Althea and me for what city folk deem the bleakness of our lives here. I am sure our urban friends wonder, if after five years of perplexity they still discuss us at all, how we can continue to endure an existence so empty, so dull. It is true that we have each other and 180 acres of unkempt Vermont upland. That is all. How can it be enough?

To this Althea and I answer that it isn't quite all and that the richness and splendor of our possessions is too great for us ever to savor it entire in what remains of our already more than half-spent lives. We have not been marooned on our hillside farm. We have espoused it. We have taken it, or it has admitted us into a partnership that grows more intimate with the passage of each day.

Only those who, like ourselves, are owned by land that they supposedly possess can understand the abiding joys of our union. The free-swimming urbanite looks with scorn upon our barnacle-like existence. He sees only a white house, somewhat in need of paint, set amid semi-successful flowerbeds and surrounded by an excess of tilted and neglected acreage. He looks from these to their smugly contented proprietors and, if he be polite, keeps his thoughts to himself. He sees none of the things that forever are before the eyes of Althea and me.

Ours is not the infatuation of folk with a new posses-sion. Neighbors whose families have dwelt here for al-most two centuries share it. The old gentleman from whom we bought our farm came back often during his few remaining years, as one visits a beloved kinsman. Each birthday, he climbed to the bald crest of our hill to look again upon the face of the dear land that had been his.

Althea and I understand in part, though we do not wholly share, the attitude of another Vermonter who said to an intimate after his wife's funeral:

"Folks think, mebby, I don't miss Marthy, but I'd ruther lost m'best five acres than her."

To the outsider, our devotion to our farm would be more comprehensible if it were to yield us negotiable produce. If we were to speak of our milk, our eggs or our vegetables and the cash they bring us, we should have a more respectful hearing. To date, our land has supplied us with an unmanageable assortment of dreams, innumerable grandiose plans, none of which we ever shall be able to fulfill completely, and a queer warm sense of intimacy and mutual dependence. These are our farm's chief yield.

Hay is the only form of physical subsistence our fields supply, yet they and our woods and our hills are more to Althea and me than just so much unproductive territory. Our land is the stage across which the year's procession marches. We have learned to know our home as men and women who live intimately together come to understand small personal significances that the outsider cannot interpret or even see.

We have shared, for five years now, our property's eccentricities of light and shade, of altering temperature and color. We have come to know its foliage and its flowers, its birds and small beasts so well that were we to sleep like Rip Van Winkle here, we should be able, on rousing, to tell by the look of our land the very week of our awakening. In time, if our partnership endures, we might be able to identify the actual day and hour.

I wish for no such slumber. Already, I am aware that time is too short for me ever to know my own land as closely as I wish. It is probably the progressive dementia of the home lover that makes each successive season, barring the mud of spring, fairer than its counterpart of earlier years. This present January holds delights for me that none of the five previous first months I have lived here has offered. Each season comes to our door like an old friend returning, dear not only for himself but for the joy of former visits that accompanies him.

All this I thought while I dressed in the chilly bedroom and I heard myself say aloud as I pulled on my boots:

"I'm getting old."

I have attained that difficult age when I admit my advancing years as though confession might delay them, yet find myself growing heated when others refer to my maturity.

Senility, I suppose, is close when a man finds himself looking ever more frequently over his shoulder; when he turns from current best sellers to books of twenty years ago, less for the present joy they bring him than for the memory of an earlier delight they re-create; when he would rather revisit familiar places than adventure into unknown, when he seeks more eagerly the company of old friends than the making of new.

The reminiscences of the elderly are dreary hearing for the young, yet I, at forty-nine, am beginning to understand how precious to their owner these may be. It is no small thing to resurrect, for even brief moments, matters that you and two or three others alone remember. It is good now and then to encounter someone with whom your own inglorious annals need not also be mute.

Three dogs waited for me in the upper hall. They followed me downstairs, panting unwarranted aspirations for a walk at this unheard-of hour. I thought, as I went

in to breakfast, how much more important since we came
to live here had grown the advent of every month.

They come back to us with none of the disheartening
marks of age our human friends display. They bring us,
each one, not only memories but raw material for future
reminiscence. Each January superimposes its own story
upon the tale of its forerunners, complicating still further a palimpsest that only Althea and I can wholly
read. We live now, not in a single month, but in the
distilled essence of five preceding Januaries and, if an
upright and godly existence wins its traditional reward
of longevity, I may live to recall not five but twenty
Januaries when that month shows its final dawn for me.

I may stand in the doorway, fifteen years hence, on
another bitter-bright morning like this and watch Black
Boy's successor and Meggy's great-great-grandchildren
plow through the new-fallen snow. I should see then,
small and clear like the vision in reversed opera glasses,
this very day and all the other like mornings that had
been added to my memory by the circling years.

I understand more clearly now why Althea and I never
have been lonely and why, as long as the unreliable gods
remain kind, we never can be.

I think that those who have rediscovered and conformed to life's essential rhythm need never know dearth
of fellowship. Here, in the home that we have made;
here, with our own land about us—the protean land that
reflects the progress of each month—Althea and I are
too close to existence itself, too intimate a part of its
flow, to know emptiness or boredom.

[ 14 ]

Men are loneliest with other men and the works of other men about them.

I went toward the dining room. The dogs, oppressed by the blighting of still another hope, padded to the kitchen to demand breakfast from Bertha, our cook. This is a process more hypnotic than peremptory. They do not ask for provender. They only sit and look until she, weary of threading a difficult course among three black, obdurate, mutely reproachful shapes, succumbs and feeds them.

Sunlight shone on china, sparkled on glass and silverware and illumined Althea, who wore the smug expression that always is hers when she gets down to breakfast ahead of me. She asked, while I ate:

"What are you going to do today?" and I recited glibly:

"Shovel the walk and burn the garbage, chop kindling, lay a new fire on the hearth, write for the rest of the morning and part of the afternoon, ski for a while and write some more and then—"

I paused. Althea said patiently:

"I know all that. It's what you do every day. I mean what do you want to do this evening? We're going to Hap's for cocktails and Mary just called up, asking us to dinner. I told her I'd let her know after I'd talked with you."

"Well," I asked, "what do you want to do?"

"There's a Grange meeting tonight," Althea pursued. "We'd rather planned on going to that and there's a social in the Center. We've been invited to that too. And we'd talked about attending the concert at the Putney School. What do you want to do?"

Such is the isolation of winter-bound Vermont where, despite the contrary testimony of New England novels, entertainment perpetually is offered the resident in infinite variety. There are moments when it seems to Althea and me that there is almost too much of it; when I feel the desire to reply to still another invitation with the retort accredited to an independent if not-too-bright Green Mountaineer of my acquaintance.

This gentleman was teaming logs down a snow smothered road and grew irked by the number of cars that tooted to pass him, entailing his withdrawal into the ditch. When a final urgent motorist appeared behind him, he kept stark in the center of the road, despite much frenzied horn-blasting. Eventually the car's driver halted, got out and ran ahead to accost my hero.

"Hey," he begged, "pull over will you? I'm in a hurry."

The teamster looked down with dignity from his perch on the log load.

"Don't know's I will," he said at last. "I've accommodated too derned many a'ready this mornin'."

"Tomorrow night," I answered, "there's the P.T.A. supper in the village and the night after I'm speaking in Townshend and we're due to have a house full for the week end. Do you really want to know what I'd like to do this evening? I'd like to have dinner here and sit in front of the fire with you, afterward, and talk a little and read a little and listen to the radio for a while. I'd like to strive for some of the loneliness and isolation city people talk about and we don't ever seem to get. I'd like to wallow in it."

"I think," Althea said, "that would be simply swell."

It still is my contention that I write here in winter-bound Vermont with less anguish and distraction than I suffered in the heart of Manhattan, yet I doubt whether close inspection of my claim sustains it. Authors forever blame their failings upon external annoyances and moan wistfully about the work they might do if they were not so afflicted. It is a comfortable alibi, but I am beginning to question its validity. Only the grave offers man absolute privacy and the opportunities there for literary composition are negligible.

The intrusions that pester me in midwinter Vermont, two miles from my nearest neighbor, are not as brusque or blatant as those Manhattan furnishes. They are insidious, but they flourish. My own house and land supply most of them.

The telephone, it is true, does furnish its share. Here in Vermont that instrument has characteristics of its own. No matter what difficulties you experience in making a call, there never seems to be any hampering of the incoming summonses. It is not a perfect, two-way device and I wish at times that I had the fortitude of one native-born Vermonter.

Shortly after he had had a telephone installed in his cottage, a neighbor dropped in and found him immersed in the literary effort of filling out a form from a mail order catalogue. The telephone was ringing persistently, but its possessor took no heed whatever.

[ 17 ]

"Alex," the caller ventured, "ain't that your number?"

"Ehyah; 'tis."

"Wal, aintcha goin' to answer it for gossakes?"

"William," said the other, looking up briefly before he bent again over his writing, "I'm busy and I had that derned thing installed for *my* convenience."

Althea, driven to distraction's verge by my windy bellowings for immunity from interruption, sends me upstairs with the promise that I shall not be disturbed this morning, at least. As far as human may, she keeps her pledge, but she cannot insulate my attic workroom against the manifold hints, persuasions, promptings that victimize me.

The stairs I climb to my haven remind me that they have needed revarnishing increasingly for two months now and that each day I have promised myself to adorn them on the morrow. My door needs replaning, too. It has sagged a trifle on its hinges and its lower edge scrapes the floor. And, if I were to get out my tools, I might also mend the curtain rod I promised to fix for Althea and put up a new shelf in the cellar and tack fresh oilcloth on the kitchen drainboards and—

Infinite opportunities for estimable, indoor enterprises present themselves if I stop to think. All of them seem more worthy, since they improve or adorn my home, than gelid pecking away at a typewriter. If I give in, if I undertake the smallest repair, my promised morning of undistracted work at my trade is shot to pieces for I spend the supposedly dedicated hours at the guilty but far more satisfactory task of making what is fair in my eyes fairer still. It is man's high pleasure to do humble services for his beloved.

Temptation does not stop there. I have only to look from my window at the outer brilliance to encounter further seduction. The sun blazes. It may be clouded this afternoon. The snow is ideal for skiing at the moment. Wind may drift it and bare the undercrust if I sit indoors all morning. Hours as calm and fine as this, so bright, so alluringly adorned with shadows, should be known as intimately as possible. This is my land. Clearly it is my privilege, even my duty, to go forth to inspect its loveliness. By the time I actually settle down to work I feel emotional exhaustion that Saint Anthony must have shared.

In common with all writers, I find lunch always is served at the most inappropriate moment. Words are coming more easily. Sentences are beginning to drop into place almost of their own accord and then I must go downstairs and eat. Thereafter, animate as well as abstract influences get between me and successful resumption of my job. I can't write with requisite zest and concentration after lunch. I am the victim of a long established habit and so are three dogs.

They sit in the hall, one gigantic and two small expectant figures, and pant at me when I come out of the dining room. Here it is afternoon and every afternoon we all go for a walk. This is the climax, the very peak of the whole day for eager spirits. Pricked ears, hopeful eyes and aspiring jaws proclaim it.

I have never understood why, with 180 acres to roam

at will, Black Boy and Meg and Dougal will not fare far unless I go along. It is not delight in my society that keeps them home, for once we are embarked on our daily enterprise, they pay me the scantest of attention. Nevertheless, none of them will take his or her requisite exercise unless it be in my technical company. This can be annoying at times, but, no doubt, it is good for me.

There is a resounding paragraph halted in the middle waiting for me upstairs. It is vain to say stalwartly to three dark and shaggy tempters "Get thee behind me" for that, I know full well, is exactly what they will do. They will scuffle up after me, if I ascend to my workroom. If I close the door upon them, they will lie beside it and make their presence audible by small whines and long, wistful inhalations. If I let them into the room, they will sit and look at me.

I endure the mute appeal as long as I may. Thought does not flow freely onto paper when one is the target for three pairs of expectant eyes. Finally I give up and as I am rushed down the stair, knee-deep in a cataract of dogs, I am grateful once again that I was born male, since I am so unable to resist passionate persuasion.

Our house is now the nucleus, the core of animation, for all our frozen woods and snow-swamped mowings. The sparse life of the winter-bound region flows in toward it. In the five years of our residence, furred and feathered creatures have grown increasingly aware of our bounty. The knowledge is pleasant to Althea and me. We feel that our neighbors are accepting us.

Birds who endure the winter here—jays and nuthatches, woodpeckers, goldfinches, chickadees—grow ever more intimately our pensioners. The bare, tormented branches of the locust trees, the shrubs and evergreens we have planted are filled each day with the flash and the glitter of wings. Gray squirrels, too, come to our feeding trays in early mornings before the house is astir and, after a night of blizzard that blew open our garage door, I found that a ruffed grouse had spent the night in the building. What he was doing abroad in snow and tempest, I have no way of knowing. Though I left the door open nightly for a week thereafter, he never returned.

As my dogs and I move away from our dwelling, the life about us grows thin and at last vanishes. An edged wind, whistling over the white backs of the drifts, and the imperceptible creeping shadows are the only movements in an arctic world.

We are ambassadors from the sole remaining province of our property that still withstands winter's *anschluss* and our time of sojourn is limited, our tethers stretch just so far. Were we to remain overnight in this baleful serenity, all of us should surely die.

This faintest spice of peril tingles in the mind and adds zest to our march. Black Boy gallops ahead in spouting clouds of flakes. I plod behind him on my skis and Dougal and Meg follow me, when they are not wallowing away from rectitude's straight trail in the hope that depressions in the drifts may lead to mice.

As I work my way uphill, beauty that only the eyes of an owner can see entire spreads itself upon my land.

# The Circling Year

The sun is in the west, as bright and chill as gold. One has no sense of transition, so faint is his heat, when moving out of light into shadow. Cold envelopes the earth, snow creaks beneath my skis and cold and snow and the westering sun lay their transforming magic upon our humble acres.

It is not a static landscape on which my eyes feed. It is a deliberate pageant, a slowly turning kaleidoscope forever altering hue and pattern as the light grows level and the shadows lengthen. The piebald hills, where stands of pine and hemlock blot the lace woven by branches of leafless trees, are steeped in a transparent, heliotrope atmosphere that is neither haze nor flagrant color. Distant mountains are the odd delft blue that only zero weather grants them. Each moment a richer, more unearthly light bathes the drifts and ultramarine wells in their hollows.

I climb and pause for breath and to savor more completely the strange and daring colors that drench the world, and climb again. Dusk has muted it all when I zigzag back downhill. The intense, incredible fires have burned to gray and blackened embers. I have seen no living thing save my dogs since first I started uphill, I have moved through a locked and barren world, but my heart is too full for loneliness to find lodgment there.

We come back into the house and the warmth and the pleasant glow of lights. Althea utters her routine objections to the clotted snow that enters with us and I go upstairs again for the best two hours' work of the day. Effort in the stinging cold has burned away inertia. It seems, too, momentarily to have clarified a chronically muddied mind. My windows now look out only on blackness. Meggy, who is in the throes of one of her periodic devotions to me, slumbers loudly on my couch. I can hear the radio playing softly downstairs and by faint cracklings I know Althea has kindled our hearth fire. I turn to my typewriter. It would shock my city friends to know how earnestly I wish long winter evenings were lengthier still. Momentarily, I have the inane idea that writing is a pleasant task.

Yet, tonight, when Althea called me to dinner, I had gone outside again. I answered her and before I chose logs from the woodshed, I paused an instant. The silence was so absolute that I could hear blood singing in my ears. The snow had found a faint luminous glow of its own under a blue-black sky whose planets and constellations were the markers, buoys and lighthouses attending the ancient course of this, our new voyage, and the keen, small wind that blew upon me might have come from the dark sea through which our craft rolled.

I looked from the stars to the bright windows of my home. Contentment that was kin to passion caught me —as always it docs—unaware. We were outward bound again, Althea and I, and whatever of good or ill the year would visit upon our miniscular fortunes, this much was sure:

We should sail the great circle together. We should raise the floral headlands of May and make a landfall on the burning coasts of October. We should return again, a year hence to this very instant, and perhaps I should stand, as now I stood, and stare at the sky and think pleasantly of food and more happily still of an evening of the serene quiet that only the long and fortunately wedded may share.

Althea called me again. I picked up my burden of logs and went eagerly in to the bitter loneliness and isolation of a snowbound Vermont night.

## CHAPTER TWO

# February

IN TIME, Althea and I may find our visits to New York worth while only because there waits, at the end of each, the joy of return to this, our own place. We shall go away from home, then, chiefly for the fun of coming back. This probability, if we dared to utter it in their presence, would scandalize our urban friends. Once, it would have seemed blasphemous to us, too.

A few years ago we should have been frightened to discover in ourselves such stodginess. We should have been certain that indifference to Manhattan's delights indicated mental and spiritual decay. Not want to go to New York? The next thing we knew, we wouldn't want to go to Heaven.

So we should have told each other. That time of self-reproach has passed. Salvation now is beyond us. Althea and I have joined those peculiarly difficult heathen who don't wish to be redeemed. We have known for too long the insidious combination of the formerly landless with soil that is their very own. It has stilled restlessness we once mistook for ambition. It has created between us and our home a sense of mutual dependence that formerly would have seemed serfdom to Althea and me.

We cherish our implicit obligations now. We revel in the knowledge that each day's passage draws us and our farm still closer together. We no longer yearn for freedom. It is as well that we do not. Freedom, as the city dweller understands it, is beyond us.

We cannot alter this singular fact. We can plan our visit weeks in advance; we can depart on a scant half-hour's notice, but it makes no difference how or when we go. We find we do not extricate ourselves entire. Part of each of us, a wistful and increasingly vital portion, remains behind.

This, I suppose, is the inevitable lot of all who possess and are possessed by land. This state, next to the cleaving of men to women, is the oldest and most compelling of unions. No longer are our old white house, our pastures and mowings and woodland sharply defined entities and we, two more. Our farm and we, through much living together, have become so intricately enmeshed that when we leave our home it is only a fragmentary parting.

Neither Althea nor I perceptibly has diminished when we appear in New York, yet we are aware how much of each of us has stayed in Vermont. For courtesy's fair sake, we confide only to each other how good it will be to get home and achieve again complete union. Were we to try to explain it to our friends, they would ask with justifiable stiffness why, if all this were so, we ever left our home at all. I doubt whether my own explanation would enlighten them.

I have a dim memory of a sybarite who always took a pinch of red pepper before he filled his wine glass.

The preliminary anguish, he held, made the subsequent burgundy taste even better. Some indefinite relative of his purpose is the chief reason why Althea and I go to New York, and this is the month we are most likely to choose for our journey.

February is not the most wholly desirable time to leave our home. We should prefer to go in late March or early April, but in that season, if you live at the end of a road like ours, you can't go anywhere at all, save on mire-clogged feet. So we plan to visit New York in February. We miss less of the year's pageant if we go then.

Of all the twelve, February is the most nearly duplicate month. One may distinguish it from January chiefly by occasional days of warmth and thaw that escape in some odd fashion from the vanguard of a still distant spring. Snow grows sodden, though you know full well that another twenty-four hours will turn it to marble. Icicles drip and our road glistens with wet. A warm, moist wind comes up the valley to lift our hearts, even though our minds justifiably reject its spell. Memory assures us that, despite the day's tender promise, we may be waist-deep in blizzard before the week is out.

Such days identify February. Otherwise, it imitates its predecessor month. It has no strong character of its own. Its rigors and its lovelinesses have a plagiaristic flavor. I have seen them all in January. I shall miss little that is uniquely precious if I go away now. I say to Althea:

"We might run down to New York—just for a day or so."

"'A day or so,'" Althea tells me out of her experience, "would hardly be worth all the trouble of going. Now would it?"

"No. I suppose not. Well, maybe we can manage to be away for a week."

"That will be nice," Althea answers carefully. "That is, it would be nice if you could keep from grumbling and wanting to go home thirty-six hours after we got to town."

"You'll want to come back yourself; you know you will."

"That may be," Althea says with a guilty look, "but you'll only make it harder by talking about it all the while."

So I promise and she pretends to believe me and we get ready to go.

It is not as simple as that. It is not merely a matter of wiring for hotel reservations, packing, leaving. We aren't any longer a couple of footloose, mobile people. We have a dependent home from which we must disentangle ourselves. We must purchase supplies for the duration of our absence. We must find someone who will come and stay with Bertha to defend her from loneliness and whatever stalwart dangers two vigorous small dogs and a monumental Newfoundland cannot repel.

We also must prepare a comprehensive list of things to be done in every possible emergency, with a supplemental directory. This last contains name, address, telephone number of our most helpful neighbor, of the plumber, the oil burner man, the electrician, the carpenter, the doctor, the veterinary, the sheriff, the lawyer, possibly even the undertaker. It takes a good deal of paper work to get us away from Vermont.

Our departure upon our holiday has none of the jocund excitement usually associated with such enterprises. Each of us secretly is aware that he or she doesn't very much want to go after all. Already, we are conscious of how much that is vital we are leaving behind. To our sentimental eyes, it seems that our home itself is reproachful and even to the gaze of the most bilious realist it would be clear that our dogs are desolate.

Our appearance in our best raiment has been depressing enough to canine hearts. Clearly, we are planning some expedition in which they will not be included. When I bring the first bag downstairs, despair becomes absolute. We not only are going away without our friends, but obviously we never are coming back. Gloomy visages, laid-back ears, prostrate bodies that emit tremendous sighs proclaim that this is the end.

There is none of the usual scramble to get into the car when we go out. Black Boy and Dougal and Meg simply sit on the porch with the look of creatures that have been left out in an all night rain. We call good-by to them. Misery has made them deaf. Our last picture, as we glance back, is of three black mourners whose woe, I have reason to believe, endures only until our car has rolled out of their view. Having seen us off in a deep pall of gloom, Meg, Dougal and Black Boy immediately pick up the joy of life where, for a little space, they had laid it down. Dogs have not the mental gifts that are mankind's proud possession. Dogs are unable continually to remind themselves how unhappy they are.

Our way to New York is six hours long, but Althea and I do not find it wearisome. Its first stage always is enlivened by the remembrance of things we meant to pack and didn't. Thereafter, we relax and let the road itself revive the recollections that it and we share. An oft-traveled thoroughfare changes in time to something more than a mere highway. It grows into a memorandum of half-forgotten, small experiences. It becomes a strand on which beads of reminiscence are strung.

We tell these as we drive along. Here is the corner at which a careering truck once nearly abolished us. Beside this clump of trees, we stopped for lunch the very day we drove with the juvenile Black Boy and the disdainful Dougal up to our new home in Vermont. Yonder is the house before which I changed a flat tire year before last. Ahead is the hill on which we skidded lamentably on a day of sleet. Once, a traffic cop caught me just beyond that corner. There is companionship in a familiar road that even the most magnificent strange highway lacks. Each passage adds a bead or so to those already on its string.

It is pleasant to measure our progress, not only by mileage, but by the shrinkage of the roadside drifts as we travel southward. We are leaving the stark Vermont winter behind us. We are coming into a land where soon it will be spring. Suddenly one of the new great traffic arteries absorbs us in its flow and pours us into the heart of New York.

We have returned to the town that was the home of each of us for more than thirty years. Immediately we feel ill at ease and alien and old. More changes than, by God's grace, Vermont will suffer in the next half century have been wrought in Manhattan during the brief space of our absence. Buildings have come down and others have soared in their stead. The whole aspect of once familiar streets has altered. The skyline has changed. Regions that once were fair have turned shabby and palatial apartment houses have risen in what we knew as slums. The adolescent growth is shocking to minds that are accustomed to Green Mountain stability. Manhattan's calm obliviousness is more distressing still. We have come from half-empty Vermont to the complete loneliness to be found only in the midst of several million persons.

Here, men are packed so closely that there is no distinguishing rim of space around any of them. Here, each mortal is an actual person to, at most, only a chemical trace of the total population. Our onetime home ignores us. No one is even remotely aware that Dummerston's Second Constable and his helpmeet have come to town and I have an unhappy suspicion that no one would care very much if the fact were made public. Suddenly, Althea and I have the feeling that we are not three-dimensional, substantial individuals any more. We are practically transparent and just barely audible.

This is chilling knowledge to folk who are acclimated to the friendly and intense regard of neighbors. We watch ourselves carefully for the first few hours of our stay. Otherwise, by acquired habit, we are likely to greet all whom we meet face to face and that is as grievous a sin in New York as it would be to ignore strangers in Vermont. We must remember that we aren't persons any more, but simply two additional unregarded integers in the city's current population.

Sooner or later, while we are here, someone is bound to ask us:

"But don't you find it rather—well, lonely in Vermont?" And he won't understand at all our consequent laughter.

If we were to try to explain it, he would not believe us and it is possible that our city-cramped egos would make our reply over-vehement. I doubt, though, even if we were deliberately to minimize the plentiful companionship we enjoy in wintry Vermont, whether our questioner would be credulous. We find ourselves in the plight of another Vermonter who yarned with an intimate about fishing. The latter boasted:

"Trollin' deep over to Champlain, last summer, an' I hooked somethin'. Landed him at last. 'Twas a three foot long bass."

"Huh, that ain't nothin'. Last time I fished the lake, I hauled up a lantern an', by Godfrey, it was still lighted."

"For God's sake, Elmer, you don't 'spect me to believe that."

"Wal, tell you what I'll do: you take eighteen inches off'n that bass an' I'll blow aout the light."

During the fourth February we spent on our farm, Althea and I drove to New York. I garaged our car and

[ 32 ]

hailed a taxicab to take us to our hotel. I recognized the driver. His stand is near the apartment house where we used to dwell.

"Well," I asked as he bore us away, "how've you been?"

"Oke," he answered. "You folks gone off on a little trip somewheres, eh?"

I didn't tell him that we had been away on a little trip of four years' duration.

We have lived too much in reputedly grim and hostile New England. We are no longer conditioned to deal expertly with Manhattan. We have grown soft. We have learned to depend upon human warmth—on neighbors who call us by our first names; on the sense of fellowship that rises from the intense concern the people of our town take in each others' affairs. That constant attention has made us feel larger and more important than actually we are. One of the salutary things about Althea's and my visits to Manhattan is the thorough fashion in which such vanity is pruned.

We are likely to overlook these difficult matters in the excitement of our arrival. Not until late that night when we have settled as comfortably as possible in the firm impersonality of a hotel bedroom do I have opportunity to brood on the changes that have been wrought in the place that was our home and in two folk who deserted it for a hill farm in the northland.

I lie in New York's equivalent of darkness and hear the city's traditional voice, that enduring, vibrant hum, unevenly spaced by the bleat of taxi horns. I sniff the odd, composite reek that is Manhattan's body odor. Sound and smell have their backward-thrusting way with me. For all that my senses can discern, the last six years might not have been. I might still be living in the city. I might still be satisfied with, or at least reconciled to, an existence so different from that which actually now is mine.

If that were so, my life would lack great, if unnegotiable, treasure. I should never have known the fathomless silence winter nights lay upon Vermont or have felt clear polar air invade my bedchamber when Althea has opened the window or have relished any of the myriad blessings, physical and spiritual, that possession of a house and a hillside have brought me. I may be a less ambitious person than he who sometimes lay wakefully thus, six years ago, and heard the clack of hoofs and the clinking bottles of the dawn-heralding milk wagon. I may be in many ways a less praiseworthy man, but I am happier and more stable.

I find myself thinking of my home and of how it must look now under the incredible February stars—the flat, pale expanse of snow, blotted by clustering trees; the walls of my house, gleaming faintly among the dark locusts; the dogs slumbering outside the door of an empty bedroom.

I am glad that Althea already is asleep. Otherwise, I might utter my thoughts and lay myself open, with humiliating promptitude, to the charge of being homesick. I must hide my affliction as long as possible from Althea's attentive eyes yet from now on, no matter how wholly we fill our sojourn with business and revelry, nostalgia forever will stalk and leap upon me without warning.

Sight of a Scottish terrier as scrubby and arrogant as my own may set me off. Then, for a demented instant, I would give Fifth Avenue's length for a crooked, uphill half mile and Black Boy gamboling before and Dougal and Meg plodding behind my skis.

I stand so long before a snow picture in a Fifty-seventh Street shop window that Althea grows impatient. I estimate the time of day by the quality of the light the artist has laid upon the drifts and wonder why I haven't had the sense to stay home—I who own the actuality itself.

In the late afternoons, I stop and gawp in rural fashion at sunlight washing the flanks of tall towers. It is not their height or their splendor that bemuses me. At this very instant, our hilltop is glowing with this same radiance. Shadows are gathering on the pasture and in the woods beyond. There is the still, tight feeling of frost in the air. Chickadees are flickering about the feeding tray for their supper and by the sharp scent of smoke I know that Althea has kindled the evening fire upon the hearth.

We have fun in New York, Althea and I. Mine is not a martyr's sojourn, yet cocktail parties and meals whose price would buy in Vermont more provender than any one man could carry on his back, shopping forays and theaters and nightclubs do not serve me as complete remedies for the bitter boredom of a Vermont winter. They are anodynes that keep me from missing it so much that

I curtail our stay in New York and flee, headlong, north-ward to embrace that boredom ahead of schedule.

Entertainment and happiness are not the same thing, though the world has confused them for unnumbered centuries.

If I watch myself carefully, I keep from telling Althea how homesick I am for my own place until the latter part of our stay and I don't mention it oftener than some three times daily, even then.

Age has a man fast, I imagine, when he discovers that his past has fallen into sundry completed volumes, bound and filed away for occasional consultation upon the shelves of his memory. Much that has been part of me is as dead now as Babylon, save for those outdated annals and the similar that stand in the mental libraries of a few who are my age.

The New Jersey village of my childhood has vanished from earth, though a spruce, brisk suburb has inherited its name. The New York that I knew is, after only six years, as wholly gone as the Sixth Avenue Elevated. The book that includes the undistinguished annals of my life, and of Althea's and my joint lives, in Manhattan is complete. I can open it now and again without wistfulness or regret. The current, still unfinished, Vermont record is more interesting to me than all its predecessors. I pray that it may not be ended while I still endure.

To my urban, former intimates, I suspect that I am a dreary and exasperating spectacle, an eloquent example of the deterioration that rural life can wreak upon a once fairly normal person. My thoughts and my speech while in the city display a disconcerting, compasslike determination to point north. I am willing, on small encouragement, to compare an unkempt Vermont farm with all the dazzle and splendor of New York to the latter's detriment. In time, I imagine, my Manhattan friends wish I were back home almost as much as I myself do.

And then, at last, comes the brave day on which we go and I have the feeling when we drive up our hill that a fractured life has been rejoined to its missing fragment, each splintered end fitting neatly with the other, and that already it is reknitting and soon will be whole once more.

Here is my own land, docile, unchanging. It will hold its present fairness when all my mortal friends are old and abhorrent of aspect. Here is the house into which after six years of adjustment Althea and I now fit as easily and comfortably as feet into old shoes. Here are our dogs, who obviously regard us as two risen from the dead, and the snow and the afternoon light upon the snow and over all the blessed quiet, the complete absence of the machine-made noise that is the twentieth century's most characteristic and plentiful product.

Althea still is unpacking when I appear in the shoepacs, heavy breeches and flannel shirt that are my normal winter wear.

"Isn't it swell to be home?" she asks and I tell her:

"Better than that. Let's not go again. We should have enough sense now to stay where we belong."

She does not argue with me, but she doesn't believe my resolution and neither, secretly, do I. All our lives, we shall go to Manhattan now and then, not chiefly for the delights the city offers, but so that, returning, we may savor to the full for a little while all the good fortune that is ours here in Vermont and the winter's depth —a place and a time, according to all the better writers, when the grisliness of life is most grimly displayed.

It is true that Hawthorne and Edith Wharton and Eugene O'Neill were unable to take into account the rocketlike rise of the sport of skiing and the transforming effect this has had on Down East winters. Skis have turned not only their owners but also a legend completely upside down. Deepening snow no longer isolates the Yankee from his fellows and leaves him nothing but his reputedly wretched thoughts for company. Snow is no affliction to the New Englander now. It is his most profitable crop. In Vermont, during February, the higher the drifts mount, the more certain we can be of companionship.

It comes voluntarily, plodding up our hill on hickory runners from dwellings down the valley. We can have as many more visitors as we possibly can desire delivered prepaid at the Brattleboro railway station merely by mailing invitations to folk in milder climes. At any other season, nothing might induce them to visit us, but if we add to our letters the outwardly mild statement that the skiing now is excellent, our friends are likely to arrive a couple of trains before the one that we have suggested.

The easier slopes of our farm have been grooved all this February by the tracks of skiis. The stiffer pitches are adorned not only with these but also with an inordinate number of bathtublike depressions. Not all these hollows fit me. There are few Vermonters who still are as inexpert on skis as I but we import guests to whom even I can feel superior.

Wintry New England's mind-warping loneliness, that has done so many strange things to sundry characters in literature, doesn't seem to have disintegrated Althea and me, though February now is near its close. It is difficult to cherish the traditional feeling of bitter isolation when, most afternoons, your farm is heavily populated by folk who flounder and fall uphill and repeatedly race down with only a vague idea where they are going and even less regard for their necks.

When the early twilight hustles in the long, bleak winter evening, I find that ordeal hard to dread. Recently demented, still breathless and snowburned men and women sit before our hearth, reordering their jostled interiors with draughts of hot buttered rum. This beverage is the liquid epitome of New England iniquity, only mildly enlivening when taken and terrifically memorable on the subsequent morning. If the current skiing craze persists, a whole set of Yankee literary cliches will have to be revised. While it endures, anyone possessing a negotiable hillside might just as well expect to be desperately alone in Grand Central Station.

This polar world, even when temporarily divested of skiers, seems neither hostile nor bleak to Althea and me. Winter now has reached the apogee of its loveliness and strange colors are abroad in the land. Blendings of sun and snow blaze up into hues of false warmth. Improbable shades of jade and aquamarine and peacock dwell in the hearts of ice columns that mark where, in milder times, a small spring dribbles down a cliff. The river's rapids are a strong dark blue where they run briefly between pearly floes.

If the days be too savagely cold for skiing, delight still dwells in them. Not the least of the joys of sub-zero weather is the conscienceless zest of thermometer readers in this region. These form a cult of barefaced mendacity and considerable power of improvisation. Their one standard is a refusal to admit that the cold has been less severe in the member's own particular locality than elsewhere. Anyone persistent enough to follow the chain of gravely uttered falsehood to a conclusion would be told of temperatures in Vermont considerably—a foot or so at least—below absolute zero.

Someone from down the valley telephones me at breakfast time, while rime still lurks about the keyhole of our front door and the dining room windows are gray with frost.

"Real snappy las' night, wa'n't it? Haow cold'd it git with you?"

For the sake of my reputation, I add a few degrees to fact but I impress my neighbor not at all.

"Only eighteen below, eh? Wal, 't'was twenty with us."

You cite that twenty when you go to Brattleboro at midday but the only response you get is a derisive snort.

"Gosh, that's like midsummer. Aout to West Brattle-boro it was twenty-six."

Further research will elicit the information that, when it was fifteen below with us and I said it was eighteen, it was not only minus twenty-six in West Brattleboro but thirty in Newfane, thirty-three in Townshend and down to forty in Jamaica. The Vermonter's local patriotism is a tender thing. He refuses to let a neighboring community outstrip his at anything.

Days of truly arctic frigidity are rare. Eighteen below, actually, is the coldest we have seen it here. Times of furious storm, when snowclouds pour past the windows like blown steam and erase all trace of our road in a few hours, are more frequent. Either rigor, though it keep us home, does not seem misfortune or even faint ordeal to Althea and me. There is intense satisfaction that is excitement's obscure relative in the mere fact that we and our house are warm, comfortable, invulnerable in the midst of desolation. We know then the comfort that can come only to those who have peril on their porch but unable to enter. With drifts lapping our doorsill, with a white desert beyond them, there is still, abiding elation in the simple fact of our immunity. Not the least joy that February brings us is the blizzard-borne sense of complete isolation that seafarers sometimes share, when worry is useless and enterprise is vain and the wise man relaxes and quietly waits until the voyage ends or the snowplow comes up his hill.

*CHAPTER THREE*

# March

MARCH IS the month when uncertainty begins to be Althea's and my daily ration. As March advances, we never ride forth without accompanying doubt. We may come back by car; we may walk ignominiously home on mire-clotted feet. During late March we accept no invitation without adding a "when, as and if" qualification. Experience with our road when spring begins and the recently iron-hard surface melts has taught us the vanity of absolute promise.

Thus, last year, we missed the wedding of a neighbor's daughter and spent otherwise the time we had dedicated to nuptial rejoicing. We sat in our most festive raiment in our car, and our car sat in a bog where our road recently had been, and after a while Herb Tuttle came along with his truck and pulled us out, but by then the marriage feast was over.

We started out for a friend's birthday party, too, vaingloriously telephoning before we departed that all signs were favorable and that, even then, we were on our way. We were on our way a long time and we never reached our destination, for our car dropped so far and so hard

into a mudhole that its battery cracked open like a soft-
boiled egg.

March is a time when little surety remains in our
world; when it is vanity to take any thought for the
morrow; when every trip we make into town is an adventure and each successful homecoming is adorned with
relief and triumph. It is also the time when we are most
acutely aware how dearly we love our own dwelling.
Each time we get back to it is a reunion after sore travail.
The frost still holds earth fast as this is written, but
Althea and I have learned from the last five Marches
that our time of ordeal has only been postponed, not
averted.

It won't be long now before we round the hairpin
turn, halfway up our hill, with earnest prayers and I
force the abused and justifiably heating engine into the
final steep ascent while Althea inhales audibly and sits
stiff and still beside me with her hands tightly clasped
in her lap, and I desperately employ what small skill
five previous Marches have brought me.

Althea's is the harder part for it is her lot to sit quiet
and endure the eccentricities of my driving without the
anodyne that, so the tale goes, stayed two gentlemen of
our acquaintance here.

These, the legend runs, drove up the West River road
to call upon a friend at his summer camp and found
there a welcome so lavish and liquid that both visitors
were not themselves when they climbed into the car
and started home.

Now, the West River road is profusely curved and the

driver whirled his car along at fifty, sixty and then seventy miles an hour. As the speedometer climbed toward eighty, his passenger made protest:

"Bill," he begged, "ain't you goin' a mite fast?" And Bill, looking at him in utter horror, gasped:

"Goddlemighty, Henry! I thought you was drivin'."

Here in Vermont, you don't merely learn to operate a car on hard pavement and drive happily ever after. There are profundities of experience and stores of painfully won wisdom still ahead of you. Your license is merely a matriculation certificate. If you are to be mobile all year in our part of the world, you must acquire the lore of winter driving, which has its own peculiar technique, and become familiar with the cognate but divergent art of negotiating spring's mud choked thoroughfares. No one of my acquaintance is perfect in either of these fields. I imagine you go on learning as long as you live.

We labor through mire, we lurch in and out of furrow-like ruts on our way uphill and at last we reach the final turn, the hallowed and heartening place in the road from which we catch the first sight of our house. Althea relaxes. She begins:

"Well, we've done—" and subsides under my brief but poisonous glare. Too often in the past, we have boasted of our success only to become dismally mired in the last boghole three rods on the wrong side of our doorway walk. It is bad enough to be stuck in the mud a mile from home. There is something peculiarly galling in such a disaster on the very threshold of accomplishment.

But when the car has pulled itself like an ailing cow through the final morass, when it halts, dripping and steaming before our dwelling, that is the time when Althea and I exult. We are back again. We have returned once more to our own place.

In such high moments, thought of inevitable woe that the future holds cannot depress us. The road will be worse the next time we traverse it. The day is at hand, and we know it, when we shall bog down completely and, leaving our extricated car on solider ground at the foot of our hill, walk to and from it until mid-April.

The prospect does not daunt us. Let the morrow care for itself. We are home again. We beam upon our house and its windows return our fond regard—or so it seems to Althea and me. We have the inane desire to go, before we unload the car, and give the white clapboards of our dwelling an affectionate pat.

All, save perhaps a few equally demented home owners will see in that impulse nothing more than a sentimental idiocy, a sagging of not-too-sound minds toward animism. Probably they will be right. A dwelling is only a specially constructed mass of inert material. Yet, if you own it, and live happily in it, Althea and I believe that it comes strangely alive.

We cannot explain how this happens. We only know that an old white structure on a Vermont hillside is an actually sentient personage to us. Our home is not merely a shelter. It is almost as intimately of our household as our son. It is not a possession but a partner.

From that mystical or maybe just plain crazy belief,

Althea and I derive security and stability and much calm delight that the city dwellers seldom know. The owners of our house, their son, even their cook and hired man are linked to each other by the community of endeavor our dwelling imposes. I think that we all share a consciousness that we are a corporation, loose, easily dissolved, but an organism nevertheless, and that our house is a symbol of our common purpose.

To our employes, our dwelling is a means to an end. Its service is their livelihood. Our house yields Althea and me no stated and negotiable return. It is true that it gives us shelter from the climate's rigors, but that is not the chief cause of our devotion. We have for our home the warm fondness mortals must feel for their dependents. Until we came here to live in our own house, Althea and I, the city-bred, had never known that odd sense of responsibility, part duty, part delight. Our dwellings in Manhattan practically ran themselves.

We were not obliged to consider their fuel supplies or to furnish them with water. Walk-shoveling, paper and garbage disposal, repairs and redecoration were matters out of our hands. We never knew the intimate routine of watching over the welfare of our residence. We called whatever flat we hired "home," but aliens actually possessed and cared for it. Before we came to Vermont to dwell, Althea and I had lived together in three New York apartments. We had fun in all of them and existence was simpler there, too, but after we had deserted each of the three, we felt no consequent pang of homesickness. Nostalgia for our own house grips us if we are away overnight.

We wonder whether those we have left in charge are caring for our home as skillfully and ardently as we ourselves attend it, and we know that, however scrupulous they may be, they cannot serve it as well. Althea and I have attained that stage of infatuation when we actually believe that we do things primarily for our house's comfort, rather than our own. We feel for our dwelling a version of the responsibility we have for our child.

Wherefore, we buy fuel not only to keep ourselves warm but also that our house may not be cold. We clothe our dwelling in fresh suits of paint and plan an endless list of improvements, a small fraction of which we accomplish, so that our home may be fairer still. Our chief reward is an aberrant feeling that we are pleasing a beloved intimate. This is not the sole return our dwelling grants us. We are paid back continually and unobtrusively in many ways.

When I wake in the morning, I savor in diluted form the same joy that is mine when I come back home again. I get up, gird on my bathrobe and go from room to room for no clearer reason than that which prompts a miser to count his hoard. When Althea wakes, I bring to her the fruits of my inspection, always with the preliminary: "You know, sometime when we can afford it—"

Other enterprises during the day may keep me from conscious consideration of our house and its excellences but evening makes me aware of them again, particularly

if it be an evening that we are to spend together—
Althea, our home and I.

Eavesdroppers, peering through our living room window on such a night, would be convinced of the dreari-
ness of our lot. Althea and I sit and read. Our dogs lie
before the fire. So we remain for calm hours. What our
pitying audience could not see would be wholly apparent to us. We are in our place. This is where we belong.
It is serenity and quiet elation for us both merely to be
in our own house.

Existence—the simple process of being—is pleasant to
folk who live like Althea and me. Our city friends overlook this fact when they deplore the bleak monotony of
our winter-bound lot. No folk of my knowledge relish
gaiety and revelry more than we, yet in this quiet place
we find them luxuries, not necessities—liqueurs at the
meal's end, not draughts that must be employed to wash
it down. We have time and space to appreciate the
usually unconsidered blessing of still sound bodies and
the calm delights of each successive day.

We have our radio, our phonograph to lessen the no-
torious tedium of long winter evenings, but seldom do
we turn to either. Books are better in this existence of
ours and not necessarily current books. I read, for choice,
volumes with which we stocked our shelves years ago
against the then implausible day when we should have
time to absorb them. They should be better books than
most of those the Brattleboro library has upon its "recently acquired" roster since their vitality has kept them
alive for years.

[ 48 ]

I have read all of Parkman in the last few months. Vermont is one of the best possible places to enjoy him. Melville I have read, too, and Butler and Borrow have been among my re-readings. My literary diet has been like my grandparents'. My way of life, save for electricity's benison, has not differed greatly from theirs. Clearly, Althea and I have slipped down the evolutionary scale. We are content in our recidivism.

We find it tranquilly pleasant merely to be alive, though we doubt whether our city friends, viewing the deliberate cadences of our existence, would concede that we were alive at all.

Each day, I look forward to the ritual of putting our dwelling to bed. When Althea and I grow sleepy, I let the dogs out for their final airing and follow them. I walk a little way along the drive and turn to look upon the lovely pattern of the lighted windows and I am stirred by the dim sight of our roof that holds back the night. Sometimes, Althea has to call me before I start to return. I report to her glibly that I have been seeing to this or that. Actually, I have been telling myself what a fine tall house is ours and how fortunate we are.

I turn down the oil burner's thermostat while Althea puts out the lights. Thereafter, she locks the door. This rite is a hangover from life in Manhattan. Evildoers are few in this part of the world and the most forsaken of these could not be hired to approach our house, unannounced and after dark, thanks to the notoriety Black Boy enjoys in our town as a man-eater.

Often drowsiness blurs the last scenes in the mild epic

of Althea's and my day, but sometimes it seems that scales suddenly fall from my eyes and I find myself avidly watching and savoring each small item of our household's going to bed. Such moments of intense illumination come to me more frequently now that I am in my fiftieth year. I am aware that I am observing a small, reiterant episode in our life here with a wistful intensity, as though my senses knew that their time was growing short and clung the more ardently to the little importances of our existence.

We go up the stair, Black Boy, Dougal, Meg, Althea and I. Sixteen feet of all sizes crowd the steps and cause a good deal of tripping and bumping by bodies large and small. Our dogs rush ahead of us into the bedchamber. They are waiting, when I turn on the light, for the biscuits that are the last of the day's benevolences. Black Boy beams and pants. Meg bounces about on her forepaws, sharp face alert. Dougal regards me with a dour expression. Clearly he believes his ration will be smaller than usual and inferior of flavor.

There is a moment of vehement crunching and a deal of subsequent search for implausible crumbs. Thereafter, the Scottish terriers go to the small adjoining cubicle that was built as a dressing room for Althea but now contains only two dog baskets, a rowing machine and a scale. Black Boy's blankets are spread in the hall before our door. He lies down and immediately slumbers so soundly that when we stumble over him he does not stir.

I am in bed and almost asleep when Althea turns off the light. The darkness momentarily rouses me. Air, chill and sweet, comes in through the window she has opened. I take delight in the incredible quiet of the wintry night. The wickerwork of the terriers' baskets creaks and is still. I hear Black Boy's heavy breathing and the hollow dog-like voice of a barred owl on the hill. Then silence falls again and my last conscious thought is a happy satisfaction that our house and Althea and I have spent another day together and, by that day's passage, have become still more nearly one.

At no time in the year's circle is our own home more peculiarly our intimate than when we raise the dismal and barren headlands of March. If calendars conformed to the actual rhythm of life, March and not January would be the first month. It is an inert and prostrate time with little to recommend it save the still distant promise of actual spring beyond another mud season.

The beauty and the austerity of snow have passed. The land, bared by the granulated and shrinking drifts, gives no visible promise of resurgent life. Our fields are as we saw them last December before the first snowfall came, save that they look shopworn and disheartened now beneath the matted rowen.

This year frost still locks them. There is a glitter of freed water in the ditches at noontide, but the nights remain cold. We shall have a late spring and while we wait our acres seem drab even to the infatuated eyes of their owners. Presently, when they grow sodden, they will look even worse, but our house is unaltered, though for Althea and me it has been mellowed further by another winter we have endured together. It stands, white and unchanged by the seasons, and against a sad-hued landscape, appears fairer than ever.

This is the time of year when there is nothing of merit to do out of doors. One cannot dig or plant, one cannot ski. We wait and, during this seemingly interminable vigil, our dwelling is our chief comfort, our sole cause for present satisfaction in our property. If it were not for our dogs, I suspect that I should remain permanently house-ridden during March, but since I am their possession rather more than they are mine, they insist even now that I walk with them daily by our traditional route —down the drive, through the barway, across the pasture and up, among trees, to the bald crest of our hill.

It is man's instinct to ennoble what he does not immediately understand. He looks toward heaven for answers to puzzles whose solutions are far more likely to lie, ignored, at his own feet. Much of religion and morality is the result of this perverse aspiration. Many of the fervid accounts of canine insight and intuition are the product of this same resolute purblindness.

A deal that I have at first considered my own dogs' special and uncanny knowledge has turned out to be, on closer inspection, less a manifestation of their mentalities than of my own stupidity.

Thus, I wondered most of this last winter how they knew so unerringly when I intended to go out at some unaccustomed hour. They would lie in the easy slumber which is a dog's enviable substitute for human boredom and never stir though I went a dozen times through the hall and to the coat closet on errands unconnected with an outdoor excursion.

I might fumble among the coats hanging in the closet; I might make a deal of noise but Dougal, Black Boy and Meg did not rouse. If, however, I really intended to go out, they were at my side, panting with eagerness, by the time I had put on my windbreaker, no matter how far away they had been or how stealthily I had donned the garment. Clearly this was thought transference. So I said and bade my friends marvel at it also.

Then, inadvertently, I came upon the true answer. There is a zipper on my windbreaker. It makes a whirring sound when I draw up the catch. This is the signal three fake mind readers have learned to understand. When I pull up the zipper, I am obviously going out and immediately they appear to go with me.

It is ordinary canine intelligence and not occult divination that inspires my dogs. Common sense is the last thing that we willingly grant to lower animals, possibly because we have so little a store of that commodity ourselves.

Watching my dogs, I marvel continually at the smug distinction man draws between the other mammals and his own praiseworthy self. On one hand, he ranges his species, God's earthly duplicates; on the other, the brutes, who live in a world of instinct. It is fortunate there is no unbiased umpire present to announce which grouping represents a more temperate and successful creation. No three human individuals, families or nations of my knowledge have evolved a smoother, more tolerant relationship than the two Scottish terriers and the Newfoundland who have included me among their intimates.

Nor is the association of Black Boy, Dougal and Meg based like most human systems upon preponderant mass and power. Meg weighs 18 pounds, Dougal 25 and Black Boy 120. In a world of brute force it is obvious that Black Boy would be leader. In the social organism my dogs have evolved, it is Meggy, smallest and mildest of the three, who most often gets what she wants.

God, among men, still favors the heaviest concentration of artillery. Force has no part whatever in Meggy's technique. Black Boy could kill her in ten seconds. He knows it and so does she. She prevails by patience and persistence and never drives or presses a point too far. She never abandons it, either, until she accomplishes her intention. She understands the malleability of the canine mind.

Neither pomp nor dignity sets Meg apart. To those who have just met her, she is the most insignificant of our dogs. Dougal has prophetic whiskers and the air of permanent indigestion most prophets wear. Black Boy is vast and filled with well-meaning and disheveling vigor. Both of them use Meg as a stooge, a butt for all canine romping, until some importance arises. Then she gets her way no matter how contrarily it runs to theirs.

Althea says that Meg is just plump. Less biased opinion would call her fat. She remains that way, however niggardly we feed her. I suspect that the hunting forays on which she embarks whenever we walk abroad must now and then have some successful conclusion.

No one ever was less aptly designed to follow the chase. Streamlining was not employed by Meggy's designer. She is squat and inadequately legged. Her hunting technique is as deplorable as her physique. When trailing a quarry, she screams. She does not utter heartening barks or melodious bayings. She sounds in her moments of highest glee like someone who is being flayed alive by a particularly clumsy skinner.

A humanitarian neighbor who called on us in our absence encountered Meg and our hired man walking down to the post-box for the mail. Our neighbor came to see us again immediately upon our return. We were aware that she had something on her mind and soon she produced it.

"I really think you ought to be told, because I know how fond you are of dogs. Your hired man beats them while you're away. Of course I didn't actually see him do it, but I passed him with the smallest of them and a little later I heard her crying—such piteous cries of pain."

"Huh?" said the accused when I asked him, though I already knew the answer. "Me hit Meg? I guess not. She just started a rabbit."

Those who know only casually the chubby little dog, whose small sharp head and unfortunate girth give her the appearance of something that peers out of a section of stove pipe, would never attribute to Meggy the qualities that actually are hers. Sometimes, viewing her comic and flibbertigibbet appearance, I forget them myself and their fresh display comes to me with a shock.

Only a few days ago, when we took our usual walk,

I watched her oppose and subdue Black Boy in her own fashion. The Newfoundland is Meg's graver problem, since Dougal has attained the peace-at-any-price age, yet she solves him deftly.

The bone Meg wanted was the femur of a deer, illegally slaughtered in our woods during November's ghastly final days. Black Boy found it. He was obviously pleased with his trove. He cavorted before Meg and Dougal with the bone in his jaws. He dared them to chase him. He begged them to envy him and growled ferocious warnings when Dougal showed passing interest. Meg ignored the Newfoundland and I think Black Boy was disappointed.

He pranced along before us like a drum major, head and tail high, his treasure clenched in his teeth. Meg trotted demurely behind, her thoughts clearly on other and higher things and presently Black Boy grew weary of ostentation. It wasn't much fun to show off to so unappreciative an audience and, besides, the bone's ends kept catching in brush and jerking his head about.

Black Boy stepped off the path to thrust his prize deep into a clump of ground pine, filing it away for future reference. He went on his way with the smug satisfaction of one who had just made a heavy savings bank deposit. Meg dawdled. She looked at the sky; she inspected an implausible scent with immense attention; she paid no heed whatever to the Newfoundland, but when he was far enough ahead, she turned aside, nuzzled in the ground pine and withdrew the bone.

Black Boy, turning to see why we were so unaccountably delayed, observed his treasure in alien jaws and straightway charged, roaring. I yelled, knowing how sure a gage of battle a bone can be, but neither he nor Meg heeded me. Black Boy bore down, bellowing of mayhem, upon the small, black person who dropped the bone and trotted out of its owner's way. Black Boy snatched it up and after a murderous glare at Meg, marched forward again, bearing his trophy. Behind me, Meg trotted. Her expression was inscrutable. It did not alter when the Newfoundland, wearying of his burden, cantered off into the woods and at last returned, empty-mouthed and obviously satisfied. When I looked back to see what Meg would do now, she had vanished.

I did not see her reappear, but Black Boy did. He stormed back along the trail, almost upsetting me in his fury. When I had recovered balance and had turned, the bone lay in the path and over it the Newfoundland stood, talking to himself, and in the middle distance Meggy lingered, looking pious.

Black Boy picked up his treasure. There was a harried glint in his eyes as he stared about him. Clearly, he was beginning to appreciate the carking responsibilities of property ownership. I do not think he yet was aware that he was certain to lose his bone, but Meggy was and so was I.

In the next half hour, I witnessed the Newfoundland's gradual but inevitable degradation by a creature not one-sixth his size. Black Boy did his best. He showed more ingenuity than I had known he possessed. He hid his bone in hollow trees, under rocks, in briar patches. He spent much time digging a grave for it and, having interred his property, pushed snow in upon it with his muzzle and then stared with a "There, I guess that will hold you," expression at Meg, who sat in the middle distance. Five minutes later, Meggy rejoined us. Her face was extremely frosty but she had the bone.

I enjoyed our walk. I suspect that Meg did too, but for Black Boy it must have been ambulatory nightmare. I watched him relapse from rage into desperation and fall from desperation into despair. At last he surrendered. When he saw Meg reappear for the eighth time, bearing what had been his own possession, he hesitated and then made believe that she was not there at all. He galloped off with false gaiety to get as quickly as possible away from the crunching sounds his conqueror made as she sat down and began work on what now was her bone. Neither the meek nor the vehement has a chance to inherit the earth when there is a persistent nuisance in the competition.

It is mid-March now and the mud season is still ahead of us. There are signs that it is imminent. The noonday sun, when it consents to shine at all, spreads a surface slime upon our road that each night's cold resolidifies. The swifter reaches of West River have freed themselves of ice and between the wan remaining floes water is flawed sapphire. The sky, too, when it is not abolished by fog, has taken—or so Althea and I insist to each other— a softer, more heart-stirring hue and it seems to us that on the haze-steeped hillside twigs of maple and poplar shine with a new, intense color.

Crows, who are silent and few during winter's depths,

are returning. Their raucous voices sound in the valley, harsh and dissonant as March itself and Althea, the romantic, insists that yesterday she heard a bluebird.

Town Meeting has been held and I have been re-elected second constable, presumably on a crime prevention platform, since no evil has been committed and no arrest has been made in my bailiwick since first I took office. I should be prouder of my inclusion on the list of town officers if my nomination had been greeted with less enduring merriment. Apparently my fellow citizens find in the spectacle of me as a policeman a perpetual jest the exact point of which escapes me.

All these matters point to the imminence of spring. It is late but it is surely on the way. Soon this ominously peaceful interlude will end. The time of mud and wrath is at hand. It may be upon us tomorrow, yet when it comes, it will bring its own compensation. Althea and I then will have more excuse to stay here and be quietly intimate with our home.

# CHAPTER FOUR

# April

MOST OF this nation's wars have been launched in April and Althea and I, knee-deep in our sixth Vermont spring, think we know why. So far, no one has paid adequate attention to the obvious relationship of mud-holes to belligerence, of highway mire to human ire. There are less profitable, though more widely exploited, fields for research.

While the majority of the nation's roads remain un-paved, peace must shiver and quake with each recurrent April. If the month and the mud were to endure for twice their present time, every spring would witness the outburst of war as vaguely purposed as Europe's and even more violent. Here, in what is probably America's most decorous and pacific precinct, popular wrath soars as the longitudinal swamps that once were thoroughfares deepen.

The very fact that Althea and I are conscious of the situation indicates its gravity. Rarely are immigrants like ourselves acutely aware of our neighbors' emotions. Vermonters are among the world's most self-controlled in-habitants. They adhere to a rigid decorum. This standard is necessary to keep the state from bursting into explosive fragments, for the outwardly impassive Green Mountaineer is innately a most vehement and violent man. He needs a stout boiler to withstand the pressure of his emotion. This he has evolved and if the rest of the nation chooses to regard his level voice and calm demeanor as evidences of a sluggish spirit, that is its privilege—and its grievous mistake.

It is only in spring that one can detect an ominous hissing about the safety valve of that boiler and realize how, under the affliction of enduring mud, a whole neighborhood is beginning to seethe. This is startling knowledge in a region where choler is practically universal, but as straitly clothed as the human body. Only gradually does the outlander gain knowledge of the scope of Vermont indignations and many of their ramifications and complexities still are hidden from me.

I have learned, though, that the east and west sides of the state, which a mountainous backbone sets apart, regard each other with something less than whole-hearted esteem—so much less, in fact, that governors must be elected alternately from either province in the interests of peace. Vermont anger is infinitely particularized, too.

Our own town is filled with the love and charity that well from noble women and valiant men who are famous for their good works and pacific natures, but I have heard of communities in which the population on one side of a hill resolutely ignored the persons, projects and public entertainments on its further slope. Even those ignorers were divided among themselves into adherents of the Grange and of the Parents-Teachers Association and the

P.T.A. was split into factions representing those who were mad at the current president and those who were not.

Occasionally, chronic Vermont wrath flares up at Town Meeting. Such a blaze is enjoyed by all concerned, participants in the row and spectators alike. Our own annual civic gathering is openly criticized and is beginning to be sparsely attended because it has not produced a single good fight in the last six years.

Otherwise, anger, however intense, seldom is openly displayed. Hypocrisy has no part in its repression. The Green Mountaineers simply maintain the modest and civilized belief that men should keep their stormier impulses away from public view.

Even when provocation is great, the old-line Vermonter is unlikely to lose his temper. In the presence of disaster, indignity, insult, he commonly keeps his head and by that retention becomes a most dangerous adversary who is qualified to turn tables upon his opponent by succinct and blighting speech.

An ancient farmer on a day of snow drove his horse and sleigh into a Vermont town. As he passed the Y.M.C.A. building, the temptation he offered was too much for youngsters lingering on its steps. The old man suddenly found himself the center of a cloud of snowballs. These exploded upon his person and smote his horse so lavishly that the animal ran away. The sleigh careered for two blocks before the outraged owner regained control. Then he reined in his still quaking steed and demanded in a quivering voice of a passer-by:

"What's that red brick building up street a ways?"

"That?" the questioned one replied. "Why that's our Young Men's Christian Association."

The ancient digested this. He said, just before he drove on:

"Hm! Hell of a success, ain't it?"

Green Mountain self-control is proof against extreme provocation, personal, political, meteorological. I have seen my neighbors endure hurricane, flood and seven years of the New Deal with no external wrath. Only when the mud season is at its glutinous worst does native patience under affliction begin to crack and flake away.

By the time my fellow townspeople begin to get visibly irate, my own rage has practically burned itself out and has half consumed me in the bargain. I am a charred and empty husk, mud smeared and smelling of spent fires.

My vocabulary is as exhausted as I. Althea no longer says nervously, "Now, please don't," when, after carrying uphill on my back the cargo from our stalled and wallowing car, I regain sufficient breath for utterance. I have learned, anyway, that speech cannot begin to compass the ghastly state of our road, of all the roads in town. I no longer compose letters to the local authorities that a remaining fragment of common sense keeps me from mailing, and I have ceased to plan reprisals so ingeniously horrid that their mere outline would have given Torquemada insomnia. I am used up, emotionally and physically, but now that my wrath has consumed itself, I begin to mark traces of its vast accumulation in my less volatile neighbors.

[ 63 ]

Vermonters, as their history proves, are not a people to endure meekly undeserved affliction. They are inured to climatic violences and suffer them patiently, but the mud season of April, though remotely a consequence of the weather, is to all of us far more intimately a matter of decaying roads, and roads are things for which human beings, specifically the town officials, are responsible. Their current state may not be man's fault but April's. It is more satisfactory, however, to blame the authorities.

Thanks, also, to the peculiar human mental slant, past ordeal is soon forgotten. No one recalls very clearly the torment of previous mud seasons. The current always is unique and peculiarly atrocious.

Drifts have shrunk to grimy ridges. Living water has resumed serenely the song in which it was interrupted months ago. The sun is warm in a hazy sky and soft wind blows up our valley. It is then, when the uninitiated would begin to search the edges of the sodden woods for the first spring blossoms, that roads become trenches of brown porridge and the ancestral mudholes resume their traditional sites.

Each year of the six I have dwelt here, the same bottomless pits reappear in April. In time one learns to recognize them all and recall at each fresh vernal meeting their individual peculiarities. It may be that the authorities cannot abolish them with the small funds at their disposal. It is just possible that Vermonters, who are a people justifiably proud of their past, regard the mudholes as a variety of state monument that obviously should be preserved.

To the historian or the sentimentalist, there may be some satisfaction in having his car plunge into the very slough that once entrapped Ethan Allen, but to most of us the advantages are imperceptible. I am aware that there is a muttering abroad in the land and I suspect that the ears of town officials are beginning to burn.

It is that much afflicted person, the Rural Free Delivery postman, who leads the mounting chorus of discontent. He sets its pitch and invents most of the phrases that the rest of us catch up and repeat with improvisations. Our postman is actually the kindliest and most generous of men, but even he can suffer just so long and still remain mute. Day in, day out he must traverse forty-odd miles of what used to be back-country road—in a plastered and dripping car as long as he can thrust it forward, on foot and lugging his mail bag when the vehicle will go no further. The torment he endures would unsettle Zeno. His pardonably enraged voice is the trumpet call that rouses less aggrieved men.

Meanwhile, over the deliquescent earth and the wretched mortals who slop and squelch through its quaking substance, there broods the tender and delicate sky of spring. Neither this nor the sun's increasing ardor nor April's silvery showers bring delight to human hearts. Celestial fairness wakes no lyrical response in us. It only foretells that the mud will be deeper still on the morrow. We begin to mutter to each other with dark and embittered airs that something ought to be done about it.

Neighbors, desperate or foolhardy enough to be abroad, halt their steaming cars side by side on the collapsing thoroughfares and exchange tales of their own particular miseries. Insurgence sours their speech.

"B'God, the ro'ds this year are worse'n ever they been. Voted plenty for 'em too last taown meetin', didn't we? Well then! We pay taxes, don't we? An' look at what we git. Time, by Godfrey, we took things into our own hands."

Selectmen now answer their telephones with apprehensive voices. Our road commissioners, unhappy men, begin to resemble Ishmael.

Like most revolutions, that which brews in our town is engined by wrath against the intolerable but is vague of remedial purpose. We cling, even at the height of our indignation, to the methods of democracy. We begin to talk about a protest meeting. Whether that gathering is to make its objections known to the Deity, to April or the selectmen no one is quite clear but we grow daily more insistent that an oppressed people should assemble themselves and Take Steps.

Enthusiasm is contagious. Each of us begins to plan the peculiarly scathing speech he intends to make. One difficulty stands in the way of a gathering of the aggrieved. Our embattled citizenry have been immobilized by mud. The roads are too far gone at present for them to mass themselves anywhere. Innumerable householders are willing to offer their dwellings as convention halls, but there are always nullifying clauses.

"Could hold the meetin' to my haouse an' welcome. Trouble is no one in his senses is goin' to try to drive up to my place naow."

"Ain't a bit of use my invitin' the folks to meet where I live. Got stuck three times in a quarter mile this mornin' myself."

Althea and I do not even offer our dwelling for a new Independence Hall. We are City People in the first place and, furthermore, our road has been decried by what is practically supreme authority. Only a few days ago, our car went so deep into mire at the foot of our hill that it required the effort of two trucks and numerous experts to replevin it. When the extraction had been performed, an elder statesman of the rescuing road crew inspected the mush filled cavity.

"B'God," said he, "I guess that's the best dinged mud-hole in all Dummerston."

Spring's calm beauty reigns above us. It has not yet descended to transform the marshy lower earth, but its magic is at work upon the hills. These now are clad in a soft haze and in the purple murk twigs on the nearer slopes glow with unlikely shades of maroon and yellow and scarlet. Only the abased and sodden soil itself still resists the vernal advance. The first of our spring bulbs have bloomed, almost unheeded, in surrounding mire. Yesterday, I found pale, disconsolate snowdrop flowers nodding by the side of what used to be our road and obviously deploring the company they were forced to keep.

Life quickens, even beneath the paralyzing embrace of mud. In the marshy valley through which our brook runs, the small, shrill frogs of spring have wakened. When twilights are mild, I hear the intense clamor of their little bells, crying the joys of life in a swamp to the unappreciative ears of excessively bemired mankind.

We have learned that a righteously aroused citizenry are not to be gainsaid. Plans for a protest meeting have not been abandoned but only postponed. When roads are passable once more, an epochal Congress is to be called to establish a Tax Payers' Association. Thereafter, fathers of the project insist, Things Will Be Different.

Apparently the prime, if unuttered, purpose of the organization is to make things hot hereafter for the already more than sufficiently tormented town authorities, who, by now, have come to be regarded in the popular mind as the malevolent authors of the prevailing mud.

I am a little sorry for the officials. All of them, actually, are men who spend much effort for inadequate pay or no pay at all in the ungrateful service of an electorate. Their sole fault may be that, after the not unwholesome fashion of Vermont, they are uxoriously wedded to economy, to stretching every dollar to its tearing point. Even this generally admirable quality now comes in for denunciation.

A neighbor, still emotionally shaken, has confided to me the substance of an interview he has had with one of our town's fathers who, at the moment, was supplying homeopathic treatment to a monumental mudhole. My neighbor called attention to the fact that the sand that was being shoveled on top of the mire was far inferior to gravel from a certain pit. The shoveler paused in his labor to retort that the recommended gravel was too expensive.

[ 68 ]

"That stuff you're pilin' in there," his critic insisted, "ain't worth a damn and you know it."

"Ehyah," the other admitted and went on shoveling. "But it only costs half as much."

The gentleman who retailed this interchange to me was by then in a mental state that thought of a projected Tax Payers' Association could not appease. Nothing would satisfy him but the immediate establishment of a soviet.

And it is a soviet or something even more radical that we inevitably should get if the mud season were to endure a few weeks longer. By the time it has reached its height, or depth, even the most patient and judicial of the citizenry have joined the simmering revolt. Intemperate speech spouts from normally firm and reticent Vermont mouths. Clearly, the fight that will be staged when roads at last permit the protestant convention to assemble will compensate in full for our regrettable series of pacific town meetings.

All of our community save the distracted authorities and the few lucky residents who dwell on paved highways are mobilized into one embattled camp. And now, when the stage is set for explosion and it appears that long stifled Green Mountain wrath will soar untrammeled, a new ally joins the hard-pressed officials. She is more than an ally; she is a rescuer, but the last minute deliverance she brings is insinuating rather than spectacular; transforming rather than overwhelming. She is the authentic, the almost unendurably delayed New England Spring.

Imperceptibly, she grants rigidity to the pocked and rutted roads. Her placid warmth now draws, not frost, but flowers from the oppressed earth. It is difficult to keep one's mind starkly fixed on revolt and reprisal when crocuses are pools of color on the lawn, when daffodils fill their cups with sunlight and tulips are in bud. The triumph of driving your car all the way up the hill and into your own dooryard washes indignation away.

It is time to rake the winter covering from flower beds. It is time to sow new grass seed. It is time to clear off the litter that four months of storm and four weeks of mire have cast about the dooryard. It is time to plan the garden. It is time to do so many exciting things that time cannot possibly be stretched to accomplish them all. There is no time whatever for relative unimportances such as a taxpayers' meeting.

The world alternately is drenched with sun and showers. Responsive earth alters each day, it almost seems each hour, and a thickening green mist hovers over the tan mowings. You can drive into Brattleboro now on the myriad urgent errands spring imposes with the practical assurance that you won't have to walk part of the way home. On such expeditions you find yourself singing a good deal and if on the way you meet a former fellow firebrand, you wave and drive hastily on and so does he. Both of you look a little shamefaced as you pass. Perhaps he recalls some of the more violent diatribes he has uttered not more than a week ago. You have a sheepish feeling that you matched his vehemence, but that does not seem important now, or even respectable.

Spring is here, the assuaging, the diverting, and the next mud season is almost a year away. When a selectman drives up to see me and, with wariness that tells me he remembers my recent embittered protests far more vividly than I do, promises that drastic repairs will be made on our road before fall, I believe him gladly and the draught I pour is not from the top shelf of the medicine cabinet where the poisons are kept.

Our town has grappled with its rage and has hidden it away, with an air of recent indecent exposure, for another eleven months. Vermonters are their temperate, carefully regulated selves again, competent to keep their passions where they belong. The least City Folks can do who admire and envy native self-control is to try to imitate it.

Frederick, our new hired man, has come to dwell in the cottage we built originally for our first employee, the barefooted and oracular Harry. Since Frederick and my son and I have the same first name, whoever summons any of us this summer will be sure of some response.

I watched this morning while Frederick, who said he knew how to do it, installed a new battery in the car. It was a task requiring more patience and far more ingenuity than is mine. Our hired man cajoled and wheedled the obdurate thing with all the tools at his command. Thanks to the resourcefulness of motor engineers, who oppose amateur repairs to their works by making these as difficult as possible, Frederick grimed his hands and strained his back and barked a knuckle, yet still the battery would not seat itself. Finally, the malevolent thing dealt him an electric shock so severe that he grunted.

Frederick straightened up, spent, grimed, bleeding and thoroughly abused. I waited, with memory of the mud season frenzy fresh in my mind, for forthcoming eloquence.

"Well now!" said Frederick whose family has dwelt for almost two centuries in this town and bent to his task again.

The years of my sojourn have brought me no whole understanding of my neighbors. I have only learned that one who seeks that comprehension must sweep overboard practically all impressions of New Englanders that have been derived from literature. This enlightenment isn't much, but its humble extent makes me a better authority than almost all the residents of forty-two states.

With so vast a weight of books against me, I know the vanity of picturing the northland Yankee, not as a dour and grim and rigid person, but as an idealist with a better than Southern state pride and a Castilian sensitivity. Once a literary formula has been established, you can't overthrow it.

You don't become aware of what actually goes on inside Vermonters at first glance or in the first months of association, which probably is why they have been lampooned by practically all our best authors. It takes time to penetrate the shell that the native has grown over his passionate spirit for the sake of his community's and his own safety. You have to live here for at least a year and endure a winter and survive the mire of late March and early April before you begin to win enlightenment.

Only by occasional and usually far briefer revelation than the mud season affords, have I grown to understand the strength and the intricacy of the mechanism that, with its fires prudently banked and its draughts closed, animates my slow spoken and deliberate neighbor.

I know that idealism is practically the last attribute the rest of the nation willingly would accord the lean, quiet farmer folk of this region, yet if it be idealism that impels men to reject immediate personal profit for the sake of dim spiritual gain, then I believe the Vermonter is an idealist, for I have seen such renunciation by many individuals since I came to live here and twice I have witnessed its mass exhibition.

It was a popular referendum that rejected the $18,000,000 parkway the New Deal planned to construct from the Massachusetts to the Canadian line. It was, more recently, the almost unanimous protest of the electorate that spurred a reluctant legislature into passing a law that means the doom of roadside signboards whose blight was spreading throughout the state. In each instance, the allegedly avaricious Yankees turned their backs upon profit for reasons no more materialistic than that Vermont might keep its loveliness unmarred.

I have changed my mind about the Yankee's much publicized stinginess, too. I have found that the disparaged passion for frugality is nothing more than the simple fact that, in a profligate nation, the Green Mountaineer who clings to his mountains has always been compelled to lead a financially straitened existence. Those who remain here esteem their way of life more highly than material riches. Those who yearn for money go elsewhere to get it. Cash is important in this region but not because it is the very flesh of a worshiped Mammon. It is a barricade against always imminent poverty and, to most Vermonters, the infinitely more dire possibility of charity.

The economies, the ostensible parsimonies at which summer people laugh are not essentially comic. They are admirable and, basically, pathetic. I laughed myself when someone told me that so-and-so had discharged his hired girl because she put so much soap in the dishwater that it could not be fed to the pig. I quoted this to a neighbor who was inveighing against the meanness of a local shyster. My friend looked at me with bewilderment:

"But," said he, "if you put too much soap in the dishwater, you *can't* feed it to the pig. It ain't good for him."

I remember, too, the aftermath of a poker game in which I had been the only non-native. After hours of penny ante, ten cent limit played with a calculation and gravity that would have done credit to Deauville's Salle de Barracat, we bade our host farewell, but before we got into our cars, we lingered in his backyard and conducted autopsy. This established that he whose hospitality we had enjoyed had been the game's big winner to the amount of ninety-seven cents. After this disclosure, there was an instant's envious silence. Then an optimist spoke.

"Wal," said he, "after all, it don't really pay him for the liquor we drunk and all them sandwiches we et."

Out of necessitous frugality and the resolution and the

laconic pride this entails has grown the legend of the Yankee's bitterness. He, so the national credo holds, is savagely intolerant of human frailty and the reprisal he visits upon the sinner is scathing. So it may be, but I am among the unsanctified who have encountered no evidence of this pharisaical vindictiveness during my years of residence here.

Hester Prynne, had she dwelt in this region, never would have been alphabetically indexed and I think the Salem witches might have lived here happily ever after, just so long as they gave their clients their money's worth. Vermonters are far more enlightened than most of their critics think they themselves are.

It is true that scarlet iniquity occasionally gravels the spectators, but such indignation almost always can be found to have been aroused by a concern for innocent folk who suffer thereby, not by any strong desire to punish the sinner.

A Vermont village, remote from my own town yet in the same county, harbors a woman who compensates for the depth of her morality by the height of her fertility and who, for years, has been producing offspring of indefinite paternity whom she has insisted that the town must help support, since she herself has had little time for gainful occupation.

The ladies of the local welfare society stood this deplorable state of affairs with admirable tolerance until the burning brand was delivered of a sixth infant. Thereupon, they banded together and sought the local physician.

Something, they told him, would have to be done. They had no wish to interfere with their erring sister but this serial presentation of little strangers for the town to support was fair neither to the infants nor the community.

"Ladies," the physician asked them, "what in heaven's name can I do about it?"

"Wal, doctor," the spokeswoman ventured, "we thought mebby you could kinda talk to her and mebby persuade her to be—er, pasteurized."

My neighbors regard misdeeds over which New England is supposed to gag with a calm and cultured philosophy. It may be that during the French and Indian Wars the Gallic attitude got lost among the Green Mountains and has stayed here ever since. The Vermonters I know best hold that iniquity which harms only the iniquitous is the perpetrator's own business, to be deplored by the righteous but to be penalized only by the Deity. It is the evildoer whose sins afflict his neighbor who is this region's pariah. Vermont's cold and tempered scorn, Vermont's blighting anathema is reserved for the cheat, the swindler who exploits the unwary.

This, too, is contrary to the national estimate of the New England character, like most Yankee actuality. My neighbors are traders by instinct and inheritance. They admire the hard bargain, legitimately conducted, and they esteem its driver, but a barbed wire fence of many strands is established between enterprise and crooked dealing and he who tries to wriggle through that frontier of honesty must endure the lacerations of public disapproval and private scorn forever after.

In this strange time, when what we thought was civilization has turned out to have been just so much figure skating on thin ice, my Yankee associates seem to me, despite their annual mud season frenzy, the sanest and most enviable of persons.

If stability and self-respect, if contentment with a chosen way of life geared to earth's circular progress and ungalled by grandiose ambition, if adherence to a balanced existence still governed by arithmetic's currently disparaged laws be evidences of enlightenment, then the rural Vermonter is the most nearly civilized of men.

Ours may be, as the summer people again will inform us this year, an archaic existence governed by tenets long outmoded. Vermonters, as their critics hold, may represent an obsolete stage in national development, a place where one state obstinately halted while the balance of the nation marched on. If this be so, I praise the Yankee foresight that inspired my neighbors to stop where and when they did.

May is upon us now. Tulips that have survived the perverse and exotic appetites of the deer are coming into bloom. Early daffodils are beginning to tarnish. Swelling and highly varnished buds on the apple trees shine in a sun that not only warms the bones but strikes deep into the heart. Myrtle warblers, hardiest of their race, already have arrived and the most adventurous of the summer people soon will be here. They and the necromancing sun will cover the essentials of this region with a fine, ephemeral gloss.

I shall miss the characteristic life of my homeland until another fall, for the Vermonter fades into the background when part-time residents appear and lay their urban polish upon the land. Not until next autumn shall I live wholly again with the people whose society I most esteem. Not until another April will my permanent neighbors and I attain that complete unity welded of misery and wrath that another mud season will bring. Perhaps, twelve months from now, if we all aren't as distractedly busy as we are at present, we actually will hold that Congress of Protest which I find now has been indefinitely postponed.

## CHAPTER FIVE

# May

THIS IS the month that we dedicate to the mysteries of birth. This is the time of year when the entire personnel of our establishment, save our cook, is absorbed in or afflicted by intense preoccupation with the enterprises of making things grow. Something beyond the calendar and catalogues inspires our fervor—or so it seems to me.

Land that has known a farm's routine for a century and a half exercises strange influence in May over even the most unagricultural occupants. Land, then, cries to be used in a still, compelling voice. It drives its owners from their accustomed, aimless outdoor pursuits into a frenzy of digging, planting, mulching, weeding. During May, life here is profoundly dislocated—or, perhaps, for a little while weather and tradition and the enthusiasm these quicken thrust us into the normal way all country folk should follow.

Whether we like it or not, we all have become gardeners or sufferers from gardening now that earth warms and spring is really here.

Sunlight, dwelling on our hill, nurses infant leaves. These spread along the slopes the pale equivalent of autumn's coloring. Trees, rewaking, reach for the faded raiment they laid off last fall. The red of maples, soft yellow of birch and poplar, bronzed twigs of ash copy in water color October's splendid oils. Shadows return to the woodland and, in the thickening foliage, warblers are uneasy, bright particles. In damp places, ferns thrust aloft their fiddleheads and moldering last year's leaves are starred by mild constellations of hepaticas. They nod in the warm south wind.

These importances are matters of only secondary moment to us now. We have had our vegetable garden plowed. This is an enterprise whose accomplishment in May when everyone wants plowing done requires a vast expenditure of influence, cajolery and diplomacy. There is an exciting smell of fresh earth about our dwelling and at its source Frederick is being instructed in garden lore after the method of Squeers by a neighbor who has been engaged for that purpose. Frederick is an obliging if unenthusiastic pupil. An ax, heretofore, has been his chief instrument of livelihood. I suspect that he secretly considers the rearing of seeds as a piddling and anemic occupation. I bide my time, waiting for the fascination to grip him as five years ago it fastened upon me.

It holds me most firmly now. May is the time of plans too large and hopes too high for even approximate fulfillment. May is the month when, with faith heretofore annually betrayed, you believe once again that what you commit to earth will bear at maturity close resemblance to the seed catalogues' descriptions and pictures.

I spend each day of May the irreducible minimum of time at my trade. It is hard to turn out copy when in my attic I receive so many incitements to infinitely more pleasant creative effort. Hoes clink in the vegetable garden. From my window I can see Althea, crouched in the pose of Moslem worship beside the iris bed. I hear her speak bitterly to the dogs, who want to help. I alone am isolated from the prevailing passion. As soon as possible, I shall break out of quarantine. Evening will find me, not spent by literary endeavor, but with a crick in my back, sore knees, hands that seem permanently grimed and a feeling of actual accomplishment to soothe my bodily ills.

Peas, sown recklessly early in the hope that just possibly this year a late frost won't get them, are sprouting now. We have begun our annual warfare with the deer. New batteries have been installed for the electric fence we have strung about our vegetable patch. This is a potent and perilous device that so far has grievously smitten every member of our household who has absent-mindedly approached its wire. The deer are less sensitive. Hardy or particularly well-insulated members of their predatory tribe continued to work their way through the fence until we mobilized our Newfoundland as a supporting force.

Black Boy's kennel now stands in the middle of our vegetable garden and I have added another chore to our ritual of going to bed. When I let the dogs out for the last time, I grapple with him and urge him to his sentry box, a task little more difficult than pushing a grand piano thither.

Black Boy has small delight in his promotion to the rank of actual watch dog. He sighs each night when I chain him like one whose best friend has played him false. Low moaning sounds follow me as I go back to the house. They smite my heart, but his presence in the garden, plus the electric fence, does keep the deer at bay. I suspect Black Boy's vigilance, however. I believe he affrights the raiders, not by bloodthirsty warnings, but characteristically flagrant snores.

Dougal, too, suffers from our gardening frenzy. Suddenly, precincts over which he has roamed at will for months past have become holy ground. Trespass upon them is the signal for intense obloquy from Dougal's human associates and, if available, a missile or so. Such things hurt our senior dog's dignity which is his most cherished possession. His whiskered face seems to grow a full two inches longer during planting time.

Meg is not embroiled this May in our dedication to birth. Meg has no interest at present in fresh loam that invites one to dig or ranks of new seedlings which even the best meaning dog can sit upon without ever seeing. She has no part in the vernal mystery. Meg, this spring, has supplied us with a mystery of her own, surpassing in wonder to me the transformation of pebbly seeds into green, sun-seeking leaves and stems.

Meg lies in a whelping box, in the alcove off the hall. Six pups nuzzle her flank and I, who last month would have told you smugly that I knew all about my dogs, am bewildered and humbled, for I have witnessed the miracle of Meggy's travail.

The quickening of vegetable or flower seed also is a matter beyond my intelligence but I know that agronomists rationalize it and evolve impenetrable formulae in support of their contentions. Possibly scientists can explain to their own satisfaction certain matters attendant upon the birth of Meg's puppies. I, who saw it, doubt whether any human exposition would enlighten me. It is the basic, the wholly elemental things of life into which the mind of man is likely to run full tilt and then stop. The natal night of our six new dogs should have brought me a certain sense of triumph. It only yielded me perplexity and a feeling of utter mental defeat.

The puppies were a problem long before they became even a future probability. Though we bought Meg as a helpmeet for Dougal, Althea for a long while kept her face firmly set against the marriage. It took a deal of argument to relax her. After twenty-odd years of union with me, my wife for some reason displayed a sudden enthusiasm for single blessedness in others. Her final surrender did not abolish the problem. It only complicated it.

After the banns had been proclaimed with Althea's reluctant consent, another dissenter got in the project's way. It was Dougal. Apparently, the condescending fondness Dougal had displayed toward Meg since her puppyhood was not uxorious. It was merely avuncular. For nine years, Dougal had led so blameless a life that piety had become chronic. His thoughts had been on higher things for so long that they had developed adhesions. His interest in Meg was entirely spiritual. It is dangerous to let even the most exalted virtue become an ingrained habit. We had to look elsewhere, to the accompaniment of renewed argument, for Meggy's spouse.

Dougal's resolute celibacy was not entirely misfortune.

His monasticism gave us the opportunity to seek for our pups a more wholly symmetrical sire. There was no reason now, I told Althea, why we should not dump sentiment overboard and by adherence to eugenics' wholesome creed evolve a litter that would yield at least one pup who looked more like a Scottish terrier than either Dougal or Meg. All we had to do was find a dog whose physical excellences compensated for Meggy's deficiencies.

Our search, Althea and I agreed, was not to be conducted in dishevelment and haste. We knew the sort of father our puppies needed. He should be a dog of sober disposition to counterbalance Meg's perpetual effervescence. He should be lean to offset her tendency to plumpness that the most rigid of diets seems unable to remedy. He should be heavy of head, lest all the children inherit their mother's charming but undeniably snipy visage.

We found him at last, a dark gentleman of impressive lineage, with the sturdy body lovers of the breed call beautiful, the face of a Jeremiah and a high reputation for gravity and probity.

Today, six small black persons who look more like miniature seal pups than Scottish terriers of proud lineage skid on rotund bellies about their whelping box and cling to her whom, until their birthnight, I thought the most transparent, the most easily read of beings.

Meg looks up at me when I stoop over the box with the same pleased expression my voice always has quickened. I wish I might return her regard equally calmly. I should like to feel again that patronizing fondness and certainty. It has gone and a humiliating wonder has replaced it.

[ 84 ]

The astounding memory of that travail still lodges in my heart. There are many questions I should like to ask Meg, lying with so complete an air of self-possession and propriety behind her nursing puppies, yet if speech were granted her, I doubt whether she could explain what I saw happen any more clearly than can I.

"Why?" is a query either of us might answer. "How?" might bring her, as it has brought me, headlong into a wall no human mind may scale.

Even those who love Meg best find in her character and conduct scant evidence of impressive mentality. She has been, when not nagging the other dogs for some obvious purpose, a gay and feather-minded little dog, an optimistic chaser of a variety of quarries from butterflies to deer, a prick-eared, bright-eyed, persistently eager small animal.

As her time drew near, she grew matronly of girth but not of heart. When she no longer was permitted to romp with the other dogs, lest posterity suffer, she fell back upon a solitaire game which she conducted, according to obscure rules of her own, with an old rubber ball. The pastime entailed a deal of grave trotting after the plaything and much pouncing.

Even as she teetered on the verge of motherhood, she remained blind to her responsibilities. Althea and I were apprehensive, not she. We sought the counsel of Hazel, our friend and neighbor, a person of long experience with dogs and eminently sound opinions concerning them, save for a wrongheaded valuation of Cockers above Scotties. Hazel was generous with her counsel—so lavish in fact that neither Althea nor I could keep it all in our minds. At last, pitying us, she promised to be present at the dire event.

This was imminent now, but Meggy didn't seem to appreciate it. The hoyden spirit continued to possess her unwieldy body. She never looked sweetly thoughtful. She did not refer with a sigh to her condition. She was perverse, too, about our preparations on her behalf, manifesting extreme distaste for the whelping box Hazel had lent us and displaying waxing enthusiasm for a woodchuck hole beyond the garden, from which we had to haul her, tail first and powdered with freshly dug loam, a half-dozen times daily.

Meg's disregard of her obvious future worried us. You simply couldn't impress her with the facts of life. She remained a brisk and foolishly merry small dog. It was we who were the more foolish.

We were unaware of that Something that was to arrive in her time of need to stay and enlighten her. Was she equally blind? Did her small mind already harbor conscious knowledge past our comprehension or did some inexplicable force lay hold upon her at the instant of her first puppy's birth and use her thereafter as its instrument?

Of this only am I sure: Through the two hours of Meg's torment, I looked upon marvel. In the crisis we had dreaded, it was she who was the competent, the skillful, the self-reliant, not Althea nor I.

One minute, I leaned pityingly over a dazed and suffering little dog. Before that minute's passage she, whom

I know better than I do most of my own species; she, whose mentality was something less than a two-year-old child's; she, who knew nothing of parturition and never had seen a puppy since she herself had ceased to be one, was caught and lifted into a realm of understanding far beyond my own.

Hers was no haphazard reaction. It was complex and swift and deft. Only long practice could have won for a human being equivalent dexterity. Meg had had no such training. Meg, as far as I can tell, had had no idea what was happening until it had happened. In the climactic instant, a compelling, terrific competence came to her.

Were Althea to dance with grace and skill on a slack wire; were my son to blast Einstein's theories, I could be no more startled and incredulous, yet wives and sons have privacies on which one may not trespass. It had not, until that astounding moment, been so with Meg. I had had her as my devotee for three years. I believed I knew every odd angle of her gay personality, her flighty virtues and laughable sins, her whims, her crochets. And now—

"Oh," cried Althea, who had been haunted for weeks by tales of cannibalistic mother dogs. "Oh, she's eating her puppy. Meggy, Meggy!"

She, who even in her distress had responded by flick of ear or stir of tail to our every word, was deaf. She paid no heed to the hand I placed upon her.

Hazel, kneeling beside the whelping box, smiled:

"It's quite all right," she said softly. "Watch. It's rather wonderful."

I saw the small, tremendous miracle. What had possessed the frivolous spirit of a headlong little dog? What had penetrated the fog of pain and outrage with strong command? Whence did Meg acquire such furious, enraptured skill? Who had taught her to strip with deft haste the birth envelope from her child, to snip the umbilical cord, to lave and rub down the black and groping atom?

No doubt, no bungling was here. Purpose dispelling the fog of pain bent her to its bidding. She no longer was the shabby and suffering beast. She held for an instant knowledge past the brains of human beings to fathom.

And then, the intense, sure activity was spent and Meg came back to the world in which her amazed owners dwelt. She was again only a dazed and troubled little dog whose eyes, looking up at me, reproached her deity after the fashion of all suffering mortals.

Five times that night, I saw that transformation repeated. Repeatedly, I watched Meggy pull herself up out of weariness and pain and become a deft tool, performing swifter, surer operations than any of her watchers could accomplish. I can explain those furious spasms of skill no more expertly now than I could then. I still have the feeling that I looked through a quickly closed peephole on a province beyond the mind of men. We call it "instinct." That is a label, not an explanation.

And now, with that drama past, there rise minor yet scarcely less puzzling sequels. These problems of conduct involve not only Meg and her children but Black Boy and Dougal as well.

During Meggy's travail, Dougal entered the delivery room. Curiosity impelled him. He came toward the whelping box and Meg heard him. She raised her head and looked upon her familiar, her companion on innumerable forays, her wrestling partner, her associate in rough and tumble melees with Black Boy. She did not growl so that any of us could hear. She merely stared and Dougal wheeled and scuttled to a far corner of the room. There he sat, until I led him out, still awed by his erstwhile playmate's power. Meg, even now, possesses it.

It works as effectively upon the gigantic Black Boy. When she faces him, he quails and backs away. For no clear reason that I can frame, the canine social order of our home has been overset and out of the downfall, the erstwhile willing stooge, the first to be rolled over in a romp, the butt of her associates' rowdy merriment, has emerged as a fearsome authority, drawing her power from no one knows where.

I can make no sure guess, yet I am fully aware that Cinderella of week before last has been transformed into Boadicea. Dougal and Black Boy feel it too. Neither even tries to argue the matter. They are thoroughly cowed and only they and Meg know why.

Neither male dog has approached the puppies in their box since I bore it down into the lower hall. Neither of them actually has seen Meggy's brood. If she is elsewhere, they keep close to the far wall when they pass through the hall; if she is there, they don't pass through the hall. They meet her calm regard, wheel about with the air of having forgotten something and retrace their steps.

Day before yesterday, I found Meg sitting on the threshold of her alcove and looking at nothing so intently that

I stared too. The hall seemed empty, but, following the direction of her eyes to the coat closet, I found Black Boy therein. His head was hidden among the hanging garments as further protection against Meggy's regard. He is six times her size, but he isn't a mother.

There is further incredibility. Last night when I prepared to dragoon Black Boy into his garden sentry box, he was absent. No amount of whistling or calling could summon him. We thought he had run away rather than spend another night in duress. At last we discovered him. He was in his detested kennel. He had committed himself rather than spend any more time in a dwelling dominated by the recently patronized and disparaged, the now terrible Meggy.

I am aware as I recite the facts in all sobriety how implausible they sound. They strain my own credulity and have ruined one of my few remaining prides. A week ago, I thought I knew all about my dogs. They have bided their time and now have presented me with a whole series of questions to which I can find no answers whatever. All I can bleat is "instinct" and "instinct" is merely the tag on the rubbish basket into which smug human minds dump matters of animal conduct that are beyond their pigeonhole set of theories and comprehensions.

"Instinct" is a label more comfortably attached to the ways of ants and bees. They are creatures too far removed from us in habit and structure ever to warrant even the beginnings of intimacy. Meg, Dougal and Black Boy are my co-vertebrates, my fellow mammalians. They are my

[ 90 ]

close relatives as well as my associates. Last week, I should have announced to anyone who would listen that if I didn't know my dogs I didn't know anything. I now have discovered that I don't know my dogs.

Meg and her owners might have chosen some less busy season in which to add six members to our household. The folk who implicitly condole with us while praising the superplacidity of our existence here should spend a week with us now, which is all that would be needed to drive Althea and me completely distracted.

With prospective puppies to care for, we should have economized on the gardens we intended to maintain this summer, but it is too late to do anything about that. Seeds, roots and corms—all the products of our last winter's planning and ordering—have arrived. The ground for their reception had been spaded before the increase in our family. It would take characters more resolute than ours to scale down our earlier intentions now.

Besides, we underestimated Meg's openhandedness. Her race inclines to Gaelic thrift and rarely produces so many pups at a litter.

With so many out-of-door enterprises peremptorily demanding immediate attention, I am stealing time from such unimportances as my own craft to get our flower gardens planted. That won't be the end of the matter, either. Additional thefts all summer long will be required for cultivation and fertilizing if our investment is not to turn into complete failure.

I go on fewer walks these days with Dougal and Black Boy, thereby confirming their impression that they are the most neglected and abused of animals. They may suffer from lack of exercise but I don't. It still is a question whether my back aches more when I crawl into bed at night or when I try to get up in the morning.

Birds are returning in all their varieties. They demand my notice but they don't get it. I am keeping scant track of their arrival at present. With gardening and puppies on my mind, few birds will get into my record book this May unless they report personally to me and ask to register.

In time, my current industry may bring its reward in an abundance of flowers about the house and in its rooms. That is what I have believed for five preceding Mays and the hope still holds. It keeps Althea and me furiously wielding trowels and dibbles. Our current plight reminds me of the two solemn Yankees with whom I fished, long ago. They were brothers and one of them bore a vast package of lunch on which their wives had collaborated. It consisted of twelve doughnuts, twelve bananas and a monstrous wedge of cheese.

After they had unwrapped their repast, there was a long silence which at last I broke.

"That," I offered, "certainly ought to stick to your ribs," and one of them, gazing sadly at the opened package, made answer:

"Ehyah, guess 'twill—if we kin live to di-gest it."

Blossoms' froth brightens the hills, flecks of stranded cloud from the spring's soft sky. The trout season has been launched by the annual slaughter of hatchery-reared innocents. Violets bloom and suns grow warmer.

Despite the insurgent indolence spring is supposed to quicken in the breast of man, all these are matters on which at present I have no time to dwell. I must get my gardens planted.

Good weather is my opportunity. Rain makes me mourn the number of brown packets of seeds not already committed to earth. Cool, bracing noons when the northwest wind blows do not invigorate me. Instead, they rouse my dread of subsequent frost. I look apprehensively at the thermometer before I go to bed and wake at night to wonder if all my tender, sprouting charges are perishing out there in the dark silence.

Even the foaming of shadblow and wild cherry is less a delight than a summons to further toil. It is time for the pre-pink spraying of my young and deer-pruned orchard. This is a task that I shall willingly transfer to Frederick hereafter, but first I must show him how it is done. So I blend lime-sulphur, arsenate of lead and nicotine and return from my task, spattered and smelling like a venerable egg.

Let poets, if they please, picture May as a pagan and alluring lass. Poets usually lurk in garrets. They scorn homes in the country. Possibly I am better acquainted with May than they. I find in its regime small trace of feminine wantonness and more than a little of the character of Simon Legree.

# CHAPTER SIX

# June

OUR DAYS now are measured by the voices of birds. The vocal pulse of the whippoorwill is the last sound Althea and I hear at night. Normally he calls, by choice and to our own good fortune, from deep in the valley and at that distance, his song is soothing. Each June, some adventurer of his race comes to serenade beneath our windows and then I must rise, fuming, and rout him with blindly thrown stones before slumber again becomes possible.

The whippoorwill is the tailpiece of each day. The robin is the chapter heading of every morrow. When darkness becomes the deep, brief blue of early dawn, I hear him begin his self-conscious caroling. Like most early risers, he must call attention to his virtue and manage, if possible, to get everyone else out of bed. Althea, who is sounder of mind and conscience than I, sleeps on, but the robin's squealing song is likely to rouse me.

Thereafter, though I keep my eyes resolutely shut while drowsiness drains away, my ears tell me how the morning progresses. When the first hermit thrush winds his horn, I know that the east has grown bright. When the woodthrush begins a tranquil chiming, it is almost sunrise.

The twittering of swallows, the bluebirds' soft voices mark the morning's progress and when the bobolink first shakes his little, flat-toned bells, I give up and get up. June is not so long that one should lie awake and inert.

Level sunlight burns on the shades of our bedroom's eastern windows. I peer blinking from a southern down the valley. Gloom still lurks there, though the sunward sides of all the ridges are golden. Smoke goes up straight from chimneys of the far, small houses, reminding me that there are dedicated folk in the world whose sense of duty makes them rise before the sun. The dew on our lawn is the powdered substance of rainbows and above its iridescence, with pied plumage brave in the light of the young day, our bobolink sings from the topmost branch of the no-account pear tree we have foreborne to chop down for his particular sake. It is the very same bobolink who has roused me for six Junes— or his avatar.

It is clear to me now that I haven't really risen to look out of the window for just a moment and then go back to bed. I am not yet enfeebled enough to turn my back upon so fresh and bright and young a world. Only a small number of such days are dropped into any man's life and I shall miss enough of this by trying to work later on without playing the sluggard now. There is something about a June morning that provokes one to footless and materially unprofitable enterprise.

Hours still must pass before breakfast. There is plenty of time for almost any vain endeavor. I might hike to

the bald top of Prospect Hill to see if the prairie larks
are nesting there again this year. I might even climb
Black Mountain and determine whether its pink lady-
slippers are in bloom. It is obvious that I shall have to go
somewhere, for my shade rattlings and blunderings
about have thoroughly wakened our dogs.

At the closed door behind which he slumbers, Dougal
snuffs and gives the small conventional growl that, I
know, will swell into ear shattering barks if it is not
heeded. I admit him and turn to dress. He enters with
an air that says, far more eloquently than any articulate
words, that the service here is simply terrible.

He waits patiently while I pull on my clothes. It is
not his grim regard that makes me hasten. Black Boy
in his sentry box has heard me get up, too, and is beginning to moan. Here, his swelling organ notes com-
plain, is a devoted dog who has spent all night guarding
young peas and sprouting beans—which is a lie, for I am
practically sure he had not batted an eye until five minutes ago—and now those whom he serves forget him,
leaving him tethered in the middle of an abhorrent garden and the day already almost half over.

If I don't hurry, he will announce his woe still more
loudly and wake Althea, who will be less vociferous but
more scathing in her comments. I get technically dressed
and Dougal and I clatter downstairs together.

Dougal scuttles past the alcove in which Meg and her
puppies still dwell. I let him out and turn to the small,
black mother who has scrambled out of the whelping
box to stand midway and irresolute between her off-

spring and me. She is suffering what, I suppose, some few male human beings but all female mammalians endure—the stringent cross-pull of desire against duty. Here I am, going for one of the walks that have been her dear delight and there are her puppies and her responsibility to them. Distress is plain on her small, foxy visage. She wavers and then climbs back into her box. I pat her and follow Dougal outside.

If I were blind and deaf, I still should know that it was June by the sweet new flavor of the air. Like atmosphere, clear, pristine, yet rich with exalting promise, must have hung over Eden when it was a brand new development. Each breath I draw as I hurry to release the increasingly protestant Black Boy makes me more grateful that I withstood—or perhaps it should be yielded to—temptation and rose so early on such a fine morning.

Dougal follows me into the vegetable garden and regards Black Boy with a superior air while I release him. Both dogs keep close to me as I return. Otherwise, they might miss the walk which pricked ears and a good deal of excess panting tell me they expect. So we go for a walk. Most of my praiseworthy deeds have been inspired by nothing higher than an unwillingness to disappoint the trusting.

There is no need to tramp over hills this morning to savor the full taste of June. It dwells in our own dooryard where the bobolink still sings. His small body grows too full of ecstasy for passive endurance. He goes up into the intense sky, still singing, and I watch him slant down at last into the mowing. His nest is there but it is not where he lights. He does not fly directly to his home but walks the last stage, hidden beneath the ripening hay to foil blundering seekers like me.

Male tree swallows in shiny blue cutaways and white vests stand on the thresholds of bird houses and gossip with their wives, who, though preoccupied, have not forsworn their interest in the vanities of this world. All day and every day while the pale eggs quicken beneath the small bodies, their authors keep their heads unsecluded. Craning from the bird box opening, they observe all that takes place upon our lawn. Recently one of them attended a cocktail party that was held principally beneath the tree to which her home is nailed. She was an abstaining but obviously interested guest.

Bluebirds, so fair of hue, so romantically tender of voice, occupy a dwelling close to the tree swallows'. I regard them with suspicion for I know their apparent meekness is just so much window dressing. Yearly during nesting time, they embroil themselves in feuds with their neighbors and unless we are vigilant, we find, some day, a tree swallows' home plundered and empty, nest material scattered on the ground about broken eggs and a bluebird perched on the roof of the conquered territory, softly whistling the glories of the Third Internationale.

A robin is nesting in a crotch of the old lilac bush, just out of reach of my dogs but an easy trove for the prowling cat who may see her before I see and abolish the cat.

We strive to keep peace within this small precinct of

earth that is wholly ours, but too often it must be enforced with a shotgun. I never take the life of cat or hawk, starling or marauding squirrel without regret and a wretched appreciation of my own ignorance. Men, by their abiding lust for slaughter, have overthrown the profoundly sane balance of natural existence, leaving efforts at regulation in the hands of well-meaning blunderers like me and occasionally even I am made aware how far into error my best intentions have carried me.

Starlings plagued us all last June. The lusty immigrants have invaded even this part of the world. They would have occupied all the bird boxes on the premises if I had not killed. Last spring, I shot at and missed a sparrow hawk that was hunting in our pasture. This year the small, bright falcons returned and were nesting in a hollow butternut before I discovered their presence. They still are here. I see the male, daily, perched in the rotting pasture elm that last year a half hundred starlings had made a convention hall. No single starling remains. Whether they were devoured or frightened off I do not know. I am only sure that at times it is well to lay down the gun and stand aside and let Nature herself do her own adjusting.

Black Boy sits beside me and rumbles in his throat. Dougal places his forepaws on my knee and his whiskered face tells me how idiotic it is to wander about my own dooryard when all June is spread before us and needs inspection. It is Dougal, not I, who decrees and directs my walk.

I follow the course that he and Black Boy take.

*The Circling Year*

Wherever they lead, we move deeper into June. The hills are dappled with infinite varieties of green. Every species of tree wears its own version of that protean color and on the tender, newly varnished foliage sunlight blazes.

Through damp glades where the last violets blossom, along cleared slopes where columbines are opening, life's flow, life's strong, sweet, drenching current bears me. Keen fragrances assail me—scent of young, dew-soaked grass, the musty smell of rotting last year's leaves, faint pungence where a fox has lately passed, aroma of pines, flavor of wet and potent earth and a far faint perfume of azalea.

My eyes are too distracted for steady contemplation. They snatch at the glitter of wings, the furtive movement of brush and grasses, the half-seen, small, alert bodies, the shine of quick water, the gleam of white where a snorting buck bounds away. Soft clamor dins in my ears. Bird voices rise above an underlying, confused chorus of chirps, chatterings, whistles, of obscure stirs and rustlings. In singular, intense enlightenment, I sense that every inch of my lately inert land is suddenly, exultantly vital, that life is rising toward the momentary fulfillment and that my heart goes with it.

Resurrection is all about me. Frost-imposed death is a legend once more. The ferment of animation, compounded by earth and sun and exquisitely dependent upon their constancy, spreads itself over fields and hills, waking triumphant, infinitely fragile voices. June brings us again the illusion of immortality. The endless small tumult stirs responsive aching in my throat that best can

[ 100 ]

be eased by adding my voice to those of my equally transitory brethren.

Probably it is as idiotic as Dougal thinks I am for an elderly and distinctly unvernal person to join the passionate chant of spring triumphant, but sometimes, when my dog is not close enough to look his scathing opinion of me, I do it for no better reason than that the world, at its utmost limit of the yearly voyage seems, as it comes about on the homeward tack, too heavily freighted with rapture for my own silence to be endurable.

We return, my dogs and I, spent and soaked with dew to a house where saner persons at last are up. Dougal and Black Boy are barred from the dwelling until they dry and I change my sodden raiment and, having breakfasted, climb to my attic workroom. There, I sit abased before my typewriter, conscious that I cannot transfer from my heart and onto paper even the faint flavor of a Vermont June morning. There is less perfect ease in writing for a living than my neighbors believe.

Six years moderate diligence at my job in rural Vermont have won me no special critical esteem, yet some of the consequences have been startling and outside the normal experience of authorship. Among them, I may list the transformation of Harry, our original hired man, into a literary character, a severing of diplomatic relations with the gentleman who used to cut my hay and the general impression among my unfamiliars in this region that since I get my work made into books—sometimes—I am a spectacle remotely akin to, though probably less satisfying than, a bearded lady or a two-headed calf.

During the earlier stages of my sojourn, I was flattered though bewildered by invitations from sundry women's clubs, with which Vermont is more than liberally supplied, urging me to appear and address their assemblies. For a long time, the essential motive behind these requests was hidden. My audiences looked upon me with obvious disappointment even before I spoke and I brought away from such gatherings an adhesive sense of communal disillusion. A large and candid emissary from still another group brought me enlightenment. Would I appear on such and such a day and address her associates? I said that I would and added:

"What would you like me to talk about?"

It seemed to her a dismaying question.

"Why goodness," she told me, "we don't care a mite. Truth is, we heard you was a author and we just wanted to see what you looked like."

Since the emissary herself was not present at my lecture, she evidently had deemed one look enough.

The impact of my writing upon some of my associates has been graver than this. When I made into books the tale of our search and discovery of a home, I included Harry, our oracular and barefooted hired man, among the characters and thereby, though I had no idea of it at the time, made our eventual parting inevitable, though I did improve my royalty statements a little.

Through me, Harry tasted for the first time the habit-forming intoxication of seeing himself in print. Like all mortals, he was enraptured. He acquired a perceptible bookish aura. He sent copies of the volumes to all his friends and acquaintances.

"I've scattered 'em," he told me once, "all the way from here to Canada."

He paid an even closer heed than I to the progress of sales and startled me profoundly one day when we were working together in the garden by announcing with pride:

"Well, I see we've gone into a second printing."

In time, I grew aware that I had made, in Harry's eyes at least, a literary personage of an excellent hired man. It was a mistake that I shall not repeat.

Neither shall I, henceforth, use as material whatever strife I have with my associates if, thereafter, I hope to use the associates. I dwelt in one book at some length but with resolute temperance on my yearly struggles with a dilatory gentleman who always promised to cut my hay on time and generally got round to it six weeks late. I might better have omitted that passage for the dilatory gentleman read it and now won't cut my hay at all. Worse than that, when we meet he glares at me and breathes hard through his nose.

He who writes of rural Vermont in rural Vermont cannot hew, with vigorous disregard, to the line. His chief concern if he hopes to continue to live comfortably there must be the size of his chips and where they fall. The dweller in this part of the world finds that he is bound to his neighbors in an endearing and infinitely enjoyable, though occasionally disconcerting, intimacy.

Althea and I are amused when summer people speak of the placidity of our existence. We hope we conceal our mirth more successfully than they hide their own complacency. Each word they utter in ostensible praise of Vermont's tranquillity reeks with sympathy for us.

We, poor folk, are cut off from the vigor, the brilliance, the exciting hues that cities afford their children. We have become acclimated to drabness. We have forgotten the stimulus one gets from swarming human contacts. Althea and I have acquired a trace of Yankee fortitude. We argue no longer with these condescending folk. We have tried it and it does no good.

We have, in the past, attempted to contest their findings. We have told our patronizing acquaintances that we, too, have lived in Manhattan and that we find our current life more sharply defined, more intensely colored than any phase of our urban existence. Then, our visitor has said with a patient smile:

"You mean the scenery. Of course that is inspiring, I suppose. But what I mean is that you lack here association with other people, knowledge of what men are doing and thinking, companionship, friendship."

"Yes, that is what I thought you meant."

"But"—there is a strain of incredulity in the question —"don't you miss all that?"

"How can we miss it when we have more of it than ever before in our lives?"

Thereafter, our would-be commiserator has given us up as hopeless. If we had pursued the matter further, if we had announced that we had learned more about more people and had acquired more friends in six years here than we could have gained during fifty in Manhattan, our visitor would have deemed us idiots, liars or both, which is apt to be the fate of anyone who speaks the truth about Vermont.

Ecstasies over communion with Nature are standard equipment for all books and articles on country existence and frequently these are penned by persons who can't tell a grackle from a starling or an elm from a hornbeam. The opportunities afforded the farm dweller for the study of his own particular species have been far less celebrated. Anyone who has lived in a small community as long as Althea and I doesn't have to search wistfully for the warmth of human association. You have to push it off your lap, now and then, if you want to get any work done.

In our town, where dwellings commonly sit in the midst of attendant fields, the surrounding space accords them and their inhabitants a definition, a three-dimensional significance no city affords. Here, about each of our neighbors is a revealing, intensifying rim of emptiness that stresses stature and heightens color.

In Manhattan we saw even our close friends only by incoherent flashes—at parties, at dinners or other revels. In Dummerston, each slight acquaintance stands out clearly against the sky and the record of all his days and deeds is set down on the immaterial yet imperishable scroll of communal recollection. This is forever at the service of the tactful seeker for knowledge and the scope and particularity of the information contained would, if

Stalin ever were to hear about it, immediately purge the comparatively inefficient O.G.P.U.

Althea's and my file of particulars about our fellow citizens still is elementary. It is only the product of a few years, yet we cherish it. There are worse and less enlightening hobbies. We have seen our dossiers grow from mere names on envelopes to plump and still swelling assemblages of items. Already, we know more about several dozen of our neighbors than all our years in New York ever taught us about any single person not of our own blood. Innumerable pictures now hang in our mental gallery. Some still are the merest sketches, others already are respectable portraits. Each day adds a new significant line, a fresh revealing dab of color to one or another.

My Manhattan friend, Richard Roe, came from some vague portion of the middle West and had an undefined position on an unnamed trade publication. I knew he was married, but I did not know to whom and I never discovered whether he had any children. He dressed well, drank dry Martinis and after the fourth was likely to sing. That is all I ever found out about him.

John Doe, my remote neighbor on the other side of our town, was born in Hardwick and moved here forty years ago. He married Elvira Blank and old Ephraim, her father, kicked up quite a row about it. John borrowed the money from old Squire Phelps to buy a farm and by now has paid back all but $321.37 of the loan. He has a daughter Bessie, who is blond and pretty and is going with young Elmer Dash, and they'll probably be married next autumn. John's son, Ora, quit high school to work for the A. and P. but he doesn't like the job and is going to resume his education next year. Mrs. Doe is quick tempered but pleasant when she isn't put out. She bakes the best pies of this region and is a power in the Grange. She is a vehement prohibitionist which is hard on John yet she's a good wife to him. He's sort of easy-going and if it wasn't for her forthrightness, he'd spend more time hunting and fishing than he should.

John was ailing for a spell last year and the doctor told him to stay indoors. The listers came to appraise his farm for taxes and John sneaked out to argue with them while Elvira wasn't noticing. When she saw him, she came right to the kitchen door and hollered, just as if all three listers and the hired man weren't there:

"John Doe, what you doin' aout there in that cold barnyard with that prostrate gland of yours?"

That is only a fragment of what already I have listed in John Doe's dossier.

With such particularized information on any person available to the collector, it follows that friendships here cannot be blindly or fortuitously contrived. Unless it actually be that human associations are warmer in this reputedly hostile portion of the nation than elsewhere, I am unable to explain why Althea and I, after comparatively brief residence, can count ourselves the infinitely fortunate possessors of more friends than were ours in New York.

By "friends" I mean, not simply those persons who hail us by our first names, but those far more special men and women to whom in time of stress we should willingly and certainly turn. There are a half-dozen such in our town and at least that number again in the surrounding region. Our devotion to them is not due merely to their magnetism or to gratitude for favors received. It is—or so it seems to us—a deeper and more essential relationship. In open spaces such as this men learn more about each other and become more important to each other than in overcrowded precincts.

Vermont is neither Utopia nor Arcady. Our sojourn here has won me, along with friends, at least a couple of fine, thumping adversaries whom I regard with full-statured detestation which they obviously reciprocate. These are not of my town but they live close enough at hand to furnish adequate and intensifying spice to existence. Althea deplores my animosity but I value it highly. Honest anger and candid detestation are too generally disparaged. The nation would be a possibly better and a certainly more entertaining place for their fuller employment.

I value more highly the friendship of one who has a few cherished feuds constantly on hand than that of him who lives in peace with everyone. The statement that a man has not an enemy in the world is no great compliment, considering that world's current composition. Enmity is a valuable personal possession. It enables me to occupy in safe and satisfactory fashion that perilous time between getting up and breakfast. Due to the enemies I have made, my dogs cringe less; Althea reproaches me more seldom. I have for my wrath a better target than any member of my own household.

Below my attic window, numerous enterprises are under way that I should enjoy infinitely more than solitary vigil. Frederick, our hired man, is working among the peas. After much scoffing, he has surrendered to the fascination of making things grow. I should like to go down and share it. Frederic, my son, has trailed away after Black Boy and Dougal who are taking him for a walk. I envy them all.

Althea has chosen the time of our elder dogs' absence to bring Meg and her rubbery, squealing brood out upon the lawn. The puppies walk small distances with the slow and stately gait of progress under water and then fall over on their muzzles. If I look any longer, I certainly shall abandon the good resolution which holds me to my task. I have enough distraction already in my mind without collecting more by looking out of my window.

I keep wondering how Bob is making out on the camping trip to Stratton Mountain that I did not join. Hap and Fred are fishing Wantastiquet Lake. I wish I felt prouder that I resisted temptation and stayed at home. I couldn't afford the time, for there's a party at Hazel's this afternoon and we've promised to attend Tess's picnic tomorrow.

I do not miss the stimulus of human contacts here in Vermont.

# CHAPTER SEVEN

# July

LONG AGO, when we had lived here only a little while, the placidity of rural Vermont began to worry Althea and me. It troubled us even while we enjoyed it. We wondered whether we should relish, year after year, such unbroken peace.

To be sure, it was pleasant to dwell for a time in tranquillity. The quiet was a blessing to ears that yearly had been outraged twenty-four hours a day, seven days a week. It is odd how thoroughly progress has ignored man's sense of hearing. Foods are pleasanter than they were a half century ago, fewer horrid sights afflict the eyes, stenches are more infrequent. Of all mortal perceptions, hearing alone has been disregarded. Vast, enduring racket is the trademark of our century.

No tumult, auditory or otherwise, affronted us in the first months of our residence here. We began to wonder whether, after a while, we should not long for just a little strife, ordeal, excitement to stir and stiffen our lives. Serenity was all very well, Althea and I told each other, but perhaps it was carried too far in Vermont. Should we not, in time, grow weary of the placid hayfootstrawfoot of the plodding nights and days? We weren't so very old. We still liked spice in our existence.

All this took place in the first of our six years here. We can smile now at our apprehensions. We have had no lack of excitement or emotional tension in the subsequent five. During these, we have endured a hurricane, two major floods and several protracted droughts. If New York can furnish equivalent upheaval, physical and spiritual, all we can say—we, who once feared that our life might seem too peaceful—is that we never encountered it during our decades of city dwelling.

Strikes and riots contrived by mere human beings are insignificant, either as spectacle or ordeal, compared to the revolts that nature can rouse, once she definitely embarks on insurgence. Urban upheaval, unless it occur in your own dwelling or place of business, affects the citizen only remotely. The countryman, when winds go wild or rivers get up or rains stubbornly refuse to fall, is caught and enveloped in the disaster. If his land is his livelihood, tragedy stalks him in the wake of the elemental insurgence. Even if his acres are only an avocation, as are Althea's and mine, the calamity marks him as well as his property.

And we, having been marked thus five times in as many years, can afford now to listen tolerantly to our urban guest's indirect praise of his own life's excitement. We feel, even while he speaks, the same mild amusement with which the elephant hunter listens to the rabbit shooter's boasting. Althea and I may not yet be veterans of climatic rebellions to which the soft city dweller is immune, but we have been at least under fire. We can show our wounds. The most painfully attained have been those that drought has dealt us.

There is spectacle to the uprising of water or wind. Sound, fury and mounting excitement all are present. Flood and hurricane are something to see and hear. Rain long withheld is a passive and gradually tightening torment. Drought, as we know it in Vermont, is not spectacular.

New England's earth bears affliction as the Yankee himself endures it, with outward calm, an unaltered countenance, a wry resolution. Beneath that apparent serenity dwells mounting tension. Hayfields, turning brown, proclaim the death of hope for a second, September mowing. Gardens crumble to dust and the innocents therein, recently so promising with blossoms, mock your dreams and labor by folding their leaves and preparing to perish. Pasture brooks dwindle and the cattle must be moved lest they die of thirst. Meanwhile, each successive sunrise stays dishearteningly clear and the warm, dry evenings are bright with stars.

None of the Dust Bowl's ghastliness attends Vermont's droughts. These are outwardly modest ordeals, more nerve straining than heart shaking. Only he who works in concert with his land for the growth of flowers or more nutritious produce feels the full force of the inconspicuous privation. A dry spell comes upon us unobtrusively and endures with no great amount of visible disaster. Frequently, it has us fast before we are wholly aware of its presence.

It is true that by the beginning of each July Althea's and my neighbors speak darkly of drought's imminence.

"Awful dry, ain't it? Need rain real bad."

Such utterances do not alarm us as much as they might. Conditions in Vermont and everywhere else where tillage is a part of each man's life always are either too dry or too wet. A week of sunshine is herald of imminent desiccation; three days of rain presage a flood.

Before the mute appeal of our own unused land woke in us the urge to plant for the financially unprofitable satisfaction of seeing things grow, I was more impatient with the plaints of agriculturists than now I am. Farmers seemed to me unpardonably querulous, resolutely dissatisfied.

I believe that the worry with which my neighbors view any variety of weather is less the product of chronic peevishness than of a neurosis to which all who are dependent upon the strenuous whims of the American climate sooner or later succumb.

This has no moderation. Even in the comparative stability of this region, the weather forever is teetering on the verge of hysterics. The man who must endure its caprices and trust to these for all or part of his daily bread is sure to acquire, within as few years of residence as mine, a case of permanent jitters.

It is true that enduring downpour only rarely is the overture to flood, yet we, remembering how storms have roused the smallest streams to incredible destruction, begin to fret if the rain lasts for more than a day or so. A week of dry weather is not necessarily the beginning of drought but that is the way it does begin and we have been parched and scorched too often not to feel dread.

Vigilance does not do the least bit of good; complaint is no more effective, yet we watch and we protest. It is rural humanity's only retort to the implacable gods.

In spite of our voluble alertness, drought steals upon us, undetected until it already is well established.

July came in this year, lush and bright. There was, it is true, promise of a scant haycrop, but that cheered rather than depressed Althea and me. When hay is plentiful, no one wants to cut ours. The prospect of a deficit meant that we should get our meadows mowed with a minimum of personal travail. I should not have to try to display the diplomacy, the patience, the ingratiation, the persuasion, the bargain-driving that the task of selling our hay frequently demands of me.

Neighbors this year actually asked for the privilege of buying our farm's chief yield. That was one miracle. We had our own peas for Fourth of July dinner. This was another. It promised to be a memorable July.

I do not know why, in Vermont, boiled salmon and green peas should be the inevitable chief substances of an orthodox Independence Day dinner and no native has been able to enlighten me further than to tell me, "Wal, we do it that way up here."

In Vermont, where "tradition" is something more than just a common noun, we do it that way, or we don't do it that way. The wise man lets it go at that.

It may be that the first peas of one's own growing and the first run of salmon up the Connecticut were Vermont's ancient harbingers of summer and, therefore, the appropriate provender for July 4th. Progress has turned the great river into an open sewer. Dams, too, have blocked the course of any salmon so lacking in self-respect as to wish to voyage its indecent waters. Our fish came from a Brattleboro chain store, but our peas were our own. Pride and a smug sense of accomplishment gave them a special savor.

Their tenderness and succulence exalted even Frederick, who had viewed the prospect of a summer spent largely in a vegetable garden with worry born of his own confessed ignorance. He had never worked at gardening. He doubted how well he would acquit himself.

Frederick obeyed the expert I engaged as his tutor with that obduracy of countenance and verbal reticence behind which the native Vermonter hides apprehension. It was not until the first peas to sprout had raised their small flat palms skyward that the fascination of gardening touched our hired man.

Our peas, thanks to the fact that late frosts were withheld, were the earliest and the most plentiful in our neighborhood. Even Frederick's late instructor in agriculture marveled at them.

"Luck," he told our hired man.

Frederick regarded him coldly.

"If you're goin' to grow peas well," he condescended, "you have to give 'em expert care."

We were blessed in our Fourth of July peas and in the presence of guests from New York who shared them.

We were fortunate, too, in the fact that the saturnalia of Independence Eve, which is another Vermont tradition, passed us by.

Those who dwell in Green Mountain villages get small sleep on the night of July 3rd and spend a large part of the subsequent holiday in retrieving misplaced belongings. The church bell is rung all night long by relays of merrymakers. The sanctioned misbehavior that prevails elsewhere on Halloween dishevels our town. Gates are removed; sign posts are twisted about; wagons, mowing machines, hayrakes are abducted and reappear at dawn in the most implausible situations.

All the long holiday, the porch of our grange building was adorned by a purloined washline from which dangled the garments of some woman so new to the region or so absent-minded that she hung out her personal laundry on July 3rd. Most of these exhibits were of an intimate nature. She did not retrieve them until kindly and concealing darkness had fallen on July 5th.

I should like to attribute our own immunity to the blameless beauty of our lives, but I suspect the credit should go to Black Boy. He is large. He is noisy. On occasion, he bites intruders and all our neighborhood knows it.

"I think," said Althea, when we went to bed on the night of July 4th, "that it's the very nicest Independence Day we've ever had. I think this is going to be the happiest summer we've spent here—but I know it will rain on all our week-end guests."

I, whom Althea accepted as a husband, should be the last to disparage her clairvoyance, but it did not rain, during July, on week ends. It did not rain at all.

We did not miss it at once. For the first time in our five years of struggle, our gardens were beginning to justify their existence. Iris and poppies had blazed against the hitherto reluctant foliage of our perennial bed and now delphinium was raising its blue banners above the foam of phlox. In the cutting garden, the stocks and the cosmos, the gladioli, calendulas, marigolds and asters that I had planted so lavishly were satisfactorily sturdy and filled with promise. We were not only going to have enough blossoms to adorn our own house this year. We were going to have plenty to give away, too.

The days went on, serenely bright. Only gradually did we become aware that there was a missing element, a repeated gap in their brilliant procession.

The air would grow sultry, the crests of the distant hills would become blurred by haze.

"There'll be a thunderstorm this evening," I would say to Althea. "Well, we're beginning to need it."

We would wake on the morrow to a cool and glittering world. The humidity had vanished. The air was diamond bright. A morning like this was the ordained successor to a night of showers, yet we had been roused by no booming tumult, no soothing rush of rain, and I could see from my bedroom window that the dust lay a shade deeper in the driveway than it had yesterday morning.

"I wish," I said to Althea, "that it would rain. Things are getting awfully dry."

"Goodness," she told me, "you fuss as much as a farmer does."

"Maybe it's infectious," I answered, but I still didn't feel at ease. In some obscure fashion the rhythm of our normal climate had been broken. We had days that presaged rain and days as fair and lucent as those that followed rain, but we didn't have any intervening downpour.

When the haymakers came and mowed our meadows and left without being afflicted by even a shower, Althea herself felt that something was wrong. Haying, with us, usually is more evocative of storm than any picnic.

We grew conscious of the beginnings of strain. We were aware of a small, increasing inner tension long before the drought perceptibly had marked anything but our spirits. We found that we had begun to pay the sky abnormal attention. There was something obdurate in its persistent clarity. We grew blind to the beauty of the herding, flat-based little summer clouds that moved slowly as grazing cattle all day long across an azure pasture. They were not the sort we wished to see. We longed for the curved and towering battlements of a thunderhead dwarfing the western mountains.

Drought comes into actual consciousness with the knowledge that life is slowing down. Drought, by the insidious retarding of growth, stresses how thoroughly the happiness of rural existence is bound to life's forward movement.

The birds are the first to feel its parched and stilling hand. Even in a moist July, bird-song diminishes, but it does not fall away as sharply as it did now. Thrushes still chanted in the dusk that brought dews so niggardly that they did not soften the grass of our lawn, but through the days few birds called. The woods, where I walked each afternoon with my dogs, were filled with sharper fragrances, the scent of baking pines, the odor distilled from brittle, fallen leaves, a smell of dust unwonted in these damp and shadowy precincts. Red-eyed vireos called from treetops with a feverish persistence that matched my own waxing anxiety and the tanager's cry seemed more than ordinarily hoarse, as though, with the rest of the world, his own throat grew dry.

The blight became visible as well as audible. Roadside brush, meek and despairing, bent ever lower beneath its weight of dust. The river's margins crept inward, pinching the flow, joining rock ledges, swarthy from long immersion, to the rim of round, pale stones that yearly are scoured by flood and bleached by sun. The stream itself no longer marched down the valley in strong and forthright curves but angled between boulders, waning, compliant. The hills still were green, but on the ridges trees whose roots lay shallow—birches, poplars—began to turn a precocious, autumnal yellow.

Meanwhile, the sky stayed bitterly clear and small clouds sailed across it. Summer people—Althea and I once shared their abased state—gloated over the perfect weather we were having. We endured their enthusiasm with acquired Vermont fortitude. Into the mutual greetings of landholders of our region new phrases had crept, eloquent of a waxing distress.

[ 119 ]

"Mornin'," we said now. "Haow's your spring holdin' aout?"

I never am able to reply to that question with full and authentic information. The most I can say is "Still running," which is all I know or wish to. Our spring flows into a vast cistern in our cellar. Each morning during protracted dry spells I go down stairs with greater trepidation than was mine the previous day. I peer into the tank through the trap door. If the water is still up to the ball valve's mouth, I ask nothing more for another twenty-four hours.

I could walk a little way uphill, lift the cover off our spring and determine how soon it is due completely to expire. I don't. More stalwart souls may be eager to learn what is going to happen tomorrow, next week, next year. I have no wish for such foresight. There is enough distress in each day of drought without drawing advances upon the future.

The prevalent ill now afflicts our lawn, that precinct upon which Althea and I have spent so much of seed, fertilizer and barbering and so much more of hope. The brittle grass bakes brown. Our spirits scorch with it. There will be no more mowing until the rains return. This would be a benison to Frederick, were it not for his knowledge that, now the grass is gone, it is certain that the vegetables in his garden stand upon the threshold of martyrdom. It is sore trial to watch the untimely demise of plants you have known intimately from birth.

Althea and I battle for the lives of the flowers that are our own particular charges. We mulch and we prune.

We scoop depressions about the stems of our more be-loved perennials and fill these thriftily with water. Fred-erick, considering the withering peas, beans and corn that are his care, glowers at our favoritism. We ignore his disapproval. Vegetables are, at best, only casual and ma-terialistic acquaintances, but the peony that you have nursed and dosed and disinfected for years is a personal friend.

So we battle to postpone what seems, as the dry, bright days succeed each other, inevitable extinction. There is more of the flavor of desperation than rescue in our labor. We may revive the palsied bergamot, we may bring new vigor to the expiring chrysanthemum, but we cannot shut our minds and hearts to the fact that all about us life that we have cherished, that has become part of our own lives, is ebbing in the malicious sunshine.

There is a still torment in the knowledge that all our farm imperceptibly is bleeding to death while the tinsel-brilliant days drive the water level lower.

He who owns land and is its partner in sundry enter-prises cannot shake himself free at will from this bond of union. The suffering of his acres becomes a personal pain, not acute but persistent. It lurks sullenly in the back of his mind. It intrudes upon his dreams. Althea and I find ourselves growing increasingly irritable as though we, too, felt our roots dry and our bodies wilt.

We still sit on the flagged platform before our front door when dusk has hidden the ravages of our ordeal. Stars are bright above us and the evening breeze erases the day's heat. In the valley a whippoorwill calls and a small breeze goes through the locust leaves. No heat lightning utters its half promise from behind the far ranges. The night is as placid and immune to distress as an undertaker's assistant. Drought has robbed Althea and me, among other things, of the pastime, dear to all countrymen, of pitying the poor folk in the sweltering city.

Momentarily, we envy them; their obliviousness to climate's afflictions, their immunity to the ebb and flow of life itself. City dwellers' sole knowledge of drought is gained from what they read in the newspapers. Life in Manhattan is a shade more pleasant for its presence. None of the open-air amusements are rained out. No ball games are postponed because of showers.

There comes a time when the sky, wearying of persistent benignity, embarks upon a campaign of celestial joking that Althea and I find additionally hard to bear. We are in no mood for whimsy, particularly of so flagrant a cat-and-mouse variety.

The sheeplike summer clouds alter in shape and hue, grow fat and dark and mendaciously portentous. We pretend not to see them. It is odd how swiftly countryfolk under stress like ours can slide abysmally into paganism. We have identified the deity in charge of the department of meteorology this summer as a saturnine god determined to thwart his people's every wish.

Althea pretends to be immensely interested in her book, but she says out of a corner of her mouth:

"Don't look now, but I think we're going to have a shower."

We keep our eyes averted from the bruised and swollen west. We talk glibly of other things.

"Thunder," Althea says suddenly. "I'm absolutely sure that was thunder."

The cloud by now has detached itself from the mountains over which it peered. It rises and it dwindles. Its lower rim is bright in the sun and beneath this there is a band of blue sky.

"Your fault," I tell Althea grimly. "You never should have mentioned it."

I rise and go to fill the watering pots again. By the time I have temporarily revived a half-dozen more swooning perennials, sunlight is all about me once more. None of its radiance creeps into my spirit.

The drought gets into everything, as a sand storm's particles intrude. It permeates all conversations. Any topic, however remote from this suffering region, inevitably finds its way back here. If you start off with Finland, you end up alongside Ed Miller's failing spring. It is only the briefest step from Franklin D. Roosevelt to Harry Tarbox and what he will do when the dwindling brook in the pasture he rents for his cattle fails entirely.

Ministers of this region determine to bring the current state of affairs to the Almighty's attention. They announce that on the forthcoming Sabbath they will pray for rain. All of us hope that such intervention will produce at least a thundershower. Some of us cherish secret doubts whether the stature of the Deity is heightened or His repute increased by the reverend gentlemen's ex-

pressed intentions. Does God pay heed only to the pleas
of self-appointed ambassadors and ignore the piercing
if less articulate petitions that an entire countryside has
been sending aloft for weeks?

Now, while trusted sources of supply begin to fail, the
dowser, the reputed identifier of subterranean springs,
becomes an important as well as a controversial personage. He strides across parched acreage with his forked
willow twig and proclaims where and how deep beneath
the surface veins of water flow. Or that, at least, is what
he pretends to do.

Many believe in his mystical craft. Their credulity
stems in part from the uneased sufferer's impulse to lay
hold upon anything, even the most fantastic anything,
that will promise relief. It is human instinct, also, to
brighten the drabness of existence by adherence to the
supernatural. Wherefore, when our farms' water systems
begin to fail, we turn for relief to the dowser, whom, in
this region, we term with a bland disregard of gender
"a water witch."

There is nothing perceptibly eldritch about our water
witches. Generally they are snuffy and shabby gentlemen
who practice their dark art with a disappointing absence of drama. Whatever magic they possess is of the
unostentatious New England variety. Even the most
pagan or insurgent Yankee hides his heterodoxy behind
a façade that conforms to the unspectacular, reticent
standards of the North East. Vermonters have acquired
self-possession, which is about all civilization can bestow

on any people and more than, to date, it has granted
most.

No shrill cries of distress rise from this tormented
countryside. Vain lamentation has small place in the
Yankee code of conduct. In times of pressure, he clings
to the saving grace of excessive understatement.

Grandma, a widow, spent her last years among her
late husband's kin in northern Vermont. There she died
and there she was buried, but the thought of her continued association with comparative strangers irked her
descendants, all of whom dwelt in a county far to the
south. Some years after Grandma's demise, the folk of
her blood decided to remove her to their own ancestral
burying ground and a grandson was sent north to super-
intend the transfer.

This was accomplished. Only afterward did doubt intrude. At a family conclave, doubt became vocal. One
asked the emissary:

"John, you're sure it was Grandma? There wa'n't no
mistake?"

"Ehyah, I'm sure."

"What makes ye so sure, John?"

"Had the coffin opened. Wouldn't move her else."

Awed silence. Then:

"You seen Grandma? John, haow'd she look?"

Another, longer silence. At last:

"Wal, not what ye'd call real rugged."

When the stress of drought gets otherwise too unbearable, you summon the water witch, agree upon his fee
and turn him loose to prowl your fields. His wizard's

wand is a Y-shaped twig. He grips its twin arms firmly in upturned fists and, with the Y's stem pointing skyward before him, stalks back and forth across your property. The indicator begins to bend. At last, as the witch moves slowly onward, it turns over completely and points toward his feet instead of his face.

There is no fraud in this. The twig definitely does turn, mysteriously, strenuously. I have seen the bark twisted off the twin arms that the dowser grips, by the force of that turning.

This inexplicable inversion of the Y-shaped wand is supposed to indicate the presence of water beneath the spot at which the stem now points. You then may summon men with shovel and pick and dig for the supposedly located vein. You may. I shan't. I lost my faith in water witches during the drought before this.

We summoned, at the height of that ordeal, a dowser of repute among the faithful. He was a personage of dignity and he marched back and forth on his mission with a high and eagle-like gait. At length, he proclaimed the discovery of a subterranean oasis. Ten feet beneath the spot he marked—or so he assured us—lay water, abundant, inexhaustible. We should dig and we would find.

We dug, persistently, profusely. In time, we created an echoing orifice in earth, so vast that it looked like something out of a Jules Verne romance. We went down fifteen feet instead of ten and came at last upon, not an ever-flowing stream, but a substance still more immortal—a gray, dry, obdurate granite ledge, one of the ribs of Vermont herself.

[ 126 ]

The water witch was nice about it. He seemed as surprised if not quite as indignant as I. Yet he clung to his prediction. He insisted that beneath the granite lay illimitable water. All we had to do was blast the obstruction away. Since there are no munition magnates in Althea's or my family, we refilled the vertical chasm instead and waited with the dull despair which patience becomes when it is held too long for the rains to fall again.

This wretchedness of the spirit is the most grievous affliction the drought brings us. It is a sullen, persistent weight upon you, more abiding than the bereavement you feel for dead plants, the anguish you share with wilted shrubs of your own planting. Each day the misery grows, walling you in more completely, shaking at last your faith in time itself.

The drought is magnified by your own woe. Your imagination cannot reach as far as its end. The glaring mornings, the afternoons' sterile clouds seem part of an eternal distress. You can recall only dimly when you and your land were not afflicted. You cannot look forward to the time when the ordeal will be over. Human optimism is just mildly elastic. It can be stretched only so far.

New England dry spells end with a minimum of spectacle. They are drama without climax, lacking a grand, uplifting finale. Here droughts wane; they are not overthrown by triumphantly marching regiments of rain.

The first showers are brief and inconsiderable. Relief at their arrival is tempered by knowledge that the frugal downpour barely has laid the dust and that beneath the darkened surface of gardens, soil still is powder dry. The second, third and subsequent rains merely ease the tension, a little at a time. Each makes us feel better, but none of them is warrant for great rejoicing.

Slowly, the lawn regains its color. Flowers that have survived lift up their heads again and the bleached and discolored ranks of the vegetable garden resume their verdant uniforms once more. Bit by bit and shade by shade, our home becomes normal. We find that we love it more deeply for the travail we have endured together, as devotion of man for woman roots in disaster they have shared rather than in joy they have known. Gradually, life resumes its old rhythms and hides beneath the small events of every day, memory of past anguish.

Urban folk who come to see us this fall will say to Althea and me:

"You had a drought last summer, didn't you?"

It was all about them, too. It ran up to the outskirts of their city, but they never noticed it.

Althea will answer: "Yes, indeed we did." She will listen politely while our guests praise the tranquillity of our life here with trite enthusiasm beneath which hides wonder how we can endure its abiding monotony, its lack of conflict and excitement.

What use would it be to try to tell them otherwise? Unless we speak to those who also live intimately with beloved land, we cannot hope to make articulate the piercing, the profound anguish and exaltation of that union.

[ 128 ]

# CHAPTER EIGHT

# August

HALF WAY down our hill this afternoon, I found myself in autumn's long shadow.

My dogs and I had been engaged upon our own peculiar version of forestry. This is a communal enterprise which includes in its scope healthful labor, improvement of my woodland, repeated narrow escapes from destruction and a good deal of unconventional shouting and running about. Were I a more expert forester several of these elements would be absent, but I doubt whether any of us would enjoy the project so much.

I wield the ax. Dougal and Black Boy furnish the audience. They sit and watch me. They are attentive but perverse for they almost always choose the exact point of observation on which a tree is most likely to come down. I can't be positive about that until the trunk leans and the wound I have hacked begins to creak. Occasionally, the tree shows every intention of falling on me. In any event, I roar when my victim starts its collapse and all three of us gallop frantically toward safety with no unanimity as to where we believe safety lies. After the crash and the ensuing drizzle of leaves, Dougal and Black Boy look at me aggrievedly and, as I start upon another tree, sit down once more in the spot of extreme danger. Their expressions tell me that they consider this an idiotic way to spend an afternoon.

Meg thinks so, too, but she has a cannier or a more impatient spirit. She never hangs around when I start to chop. She vanishes into the woods, hot on some hypothetical trail. When I pause for breath I can hear, afar, piercing squeals. These voice her hope that, this time and at last, she is about to drag down a buck of stature.

Zest for the chase has waxed in Meggy now that she has laid maternity aside. She is wiser than most so-called higher animals. She was tender and assiduous while the need remained, but she never considered her motherhood as anything more than temporary avocation. Her pups have been weaned. They dwell, when we do not let them walk abroad with us, in a wired enclosure. Meg has done her job. Her children need her no longer, nor she them. The world is filled with more than adequate compensations for that alienation and Meggy pursues these at the top of her lungs.

I think our deer get a deal of amusement out of these huntings. I suspect that rabbits and squirrels share the mirth, for the plump little dog brings back from her vociferous forays nothing material save her breathless and disheveled self. She reappears only when she thinks it is time to go home and her look, if she finds me chopping, says explicitly:

"Good heavens! Are you still at that imbecile job?"

I pay no heed to my three dogs' opinion of my industry. However illogical it may seem to them, I am performing work blessed by the county farm bureau and additionally sanctified by the New Deal. By felling horn-beam, gray birch and soft maple, I am affording arrow-straight ashes, young oaks and sugar maples their rightful places in the sun.

By abolishing what we term "weed trees," I grant the righteous *lebensraum*. I girdle, too, vast beeches and black birches, though never without an inner qualm. They have been too worthless for earlier lumbermen to take them and their spreading branches hold back, after the fashion of the aged, the growth of worthier and more youthful trees.

At behest of the government, I am selfishly improving my own woodland for my own possible future benefit. I get healthful exercise and the knowledge that I am increasing the value of my property—should I ever wish to sell or lumber it—out of labor that my dogs deem idiotic.

I am getting more than that, thanks to the inscrutable dictates of Washington. My ax is increasing the worth of my land. This, the New Deal holds, is not enough. It will pay me approximately four dollars an acre for ridding my woods of weed trees for my own eventual profit.

Zeke, a youth whose neighbors considered him af-flicted by God, appeared in his town's bakery and after staring at the wares upon the counter, displayed a nickel and ordered three doughnuts. While the baker was putting these in a bag, Zeke's unstable perception dis-covered that five cents would buy six cookies. He rejected the doughnuts and ordered cookies instead and, receiving them, started from the store.

"Hol' on, Zeke," the baker begged. "Them cookies are a nickel."

"They ain't either," Zeke returned with dignity. "I traded them doughnuts for these here cookies."

"I know," the baker persisted, "but you didn't pay for the doughnuts."

"Why should I?" Zeke answered with indignation. "I didn't eat them doughnuts."

It may be only my impenetrability to political mathematics that makes me believe that Zeke properly belongs in Washington. There must be a place for him in the Department of Agriculture.

I wish federal logic extended beyond paying me to improve my own woods. I should like to be rewarded as generously for clearing desk drawers that are crammed with "weed manuscripts." Farmers are more fortunate than authors, chiefly I think, because they have learned how to screech their woes in unison. There are treasonable moments when I suspect that my dogs' opinion of my current endeavor is more moral than the Farm Bureau's and the federal government's.

I was returning today from my profitable exercise when I walked deep into autumn. The sense of ease and the calm glee that only men who work their bodies hard ever savor completely possessed me. I felt my bones had been polished and my joints freshly oiled. Sweat and serenity are more closely allied than any poet ever has admitted and, besides, now that I am forty-nine, accomplishment of worthy physical labor is an adventure and a reassurance. When you have swung an ax for an hour or so and feel better for it, the eternal nagging fear is thrust momentarily into the background. You aren't, a gloating inner voice tells you, completely decrepit yet, anyway.

I was listening so intently to that comforting testimony, as I came down the hill, that I was aware only belatedly that the pattern of the world stealthily had changed. It is hard to describe the transformation. It was a matter of spirit rather than substance. I stopped and peered along my woodland's brief and haphazard colonnades. They had not changed, save for shifting of shadows, since I had climbed the hill. It was the atmosphere that had altered. The air had new flavor which muted all sounds save those that stressed the silence. I heard a peewee's lament and the speech of my brook on the ledges, but these only deepened the melancholy quiet as flecks on plate glass call attention to surrounding transparency. In the clearing where the cattle come to drink snakeroot lifted white froth beside the water and sunlight, dwelling on a clump of goldenrod, doubled its brave color.

I stood a long while, listening to the little voices of bird and brook, feeling and wondering at the texture of the stillness. Pleasure and melancholy were matched therein and the spell itself was piercingly familiar.

I found myself resenting it. The air was warm, the sun was bright, the leaves about me were uniform green. By all these and by the calendar itself, it still was summer, but I knew, even as I held them fast, how empty were these assurances. I stood, disquieted, in the actual silence and presence of autumn, visiting briefly her prospective domain. The summer was ending, though only the changed and muted atmosphere and the heaviness about my heart proclaimed it.

I followed a dim woodroad through shadow up into the glare and heat of the pasture and I wondered as I tramped homeward why the fall's first sign should turn me faintly downcast. Vermont was loveliest in the autumn and beyond October's splendor and November's austerity lay the peace and isolation of winter that are dear to Althea and me. It was strange that I should look backward now, uneasily, instead of forward.

Goldenrod was thick along our driveway and sun-flowers, self-sown in our vegetable garden, leaned over its fence as I climbed the hill. I wondered for the thousandth time why seed of our tender planting and constant care would not flourish so flagrantly. Althea was working in our perennial bed. She hailed me and I told her:

"The summer's about over. It feels like autumn."

"It doesn't," said Althea indignantly. "It can't. Why, only yesterday it was spring."

"It's the last of August," I answered. She looked at me with the indignation of the unjustly deprived.

"Then how," she demanded, "has the summer passed so quickly?"

"I wish I knew," I said. "It's not quite fair, is it?"

I think it is that very sense of injustice, of being obscurely shortchanged, that most depresses folk of Althea's and my ages when earth in its voyage reaches back toward the still faraway beginning of another year. Each season, when you are nearly fifty, seems briefer than its predecessor. Forty years ago, summer was an aeon long an era so spacious that the prospect of school at its far end was as unworthy of anticipation as Judgment Day. Steadily, as I have aged, the time dimension has shrunk, until now summer passes in a blur of speed, leaving in its wake dismay, breathlessness and a sense of grievance.

It is almost over. Where have its months gone? Where are all the enterprises, the small improvements and beautifications Althea and I have planned for our home? Summer wanes and not half of them have been accomplished. We shall not have so very many more growing seasons to enjoy together—she and our land and our house and I. It would be kinder—we even think it would be a little fairer—if the days marched more slowly for the elderly than they do for the very young. When the treasure grows light in your purse, it is best to spend its remnant as deliberately as possible.

It is true that autumn is not with us yet. It was a premonition, not her actual presence that I met in the woods today. When she does appear, we shall find ourselves clinging to her as firmly and as vainly as now we hold fast to summer. And the fall, too, will flash by for all our passionate efforts at delay, as a handful of dry sand trickles out through clenched fingers, more swiftly because you try to hold it tightly.

If we had not been so intent upon our own small affairs,

if we had not been so engrossed in the trumpery outdoor projects that are infinitely dear to us, realization of autumn's imminence would not have been so much of a shock to Althea and me. There have been signs that it was drawing near.

Foremost of these has been the flourishing condition of our cutting garden and its promise of bounteous blossoming in a few weeks. Five years' experience has taught us that the flowers we have planted to adorn our household never become satisfactorily plentiful until just before the first killing frost.

No matter how early we plant our marigolds, snapdragons, asters and stocks, they sprout with reluctance and grow with maddening deliberation until late August. Then, having received our mulches, our fertilizers, our repeated waterings with indifference all summer long, they gather themselves together and begin to grow furiously, as a runner sprints when the finish line is close. Each plant adorns itself with buds. The first blossoms appear. By the time Althea and I find it easy to cut a respectable bouquet without intensive search, frost descends and blackens verdant promise.

Frost never leaves us early enough or returns sufficiently late for our annuals to be completely satisfactory. Theirs are like the lives of most men—an excess of preparation for and struggle toward something that never quite happens.

There have been other animate warnings of fall's advent. The birds have been foretelling it for weeks.

Althea and I should have known when the downy

woodpecker brought his first sooty fledgling to the suet rack that summer was waning. Four generations of his tribe have been fed from that free lunch counter. Undoubtedly, by now it is regarded as a woodpecker heirloom. Althea looks with particular fondness on the downy and his children for they exemplify stalwart avian feminism.

No other female bird, to my knowledge, leaves the care and feeding of infants so wholly to father. I cannot tell how mother occupies herself when the eggs have been hatched and her brood has learned the rudiments of flight. It may be that she lectures far and wide on home economics.

I do know, though, that the youthful downy who clings to the rack and squeaks plaintively for suet crumbs always is accompanied and served by his male parent. Father is worn and dingy. His plumage is soiled, his proud red crown has faded to a dirty crimson. I think I see, too, a desperate look in his eye as though he had discovered along with uncounted millions of his sex, that the readjustments demanded by marriage are onerous and oppressive.

Yet, next spring, with a brave new suit of black and white and a passionately glowing tuft of scarlet, he will scuttle with harsh clamor up a locust trunk in pursuit of a wife once more. The pattern of life is dismayingly constant for all its possessors.

Bird-song, too, has ceased, now that romance has been wholly spent, until another spring rolls around. Before the mid-August rain, hermit thrushes still chanted at dawn and sunset. Downpour has silenced them. At dusk, the whippoorwill still calls, but briefly and unevenly, as though the mechanism that had kept him persistently vocal each night since April at last were running down.

The time of rugged individualism is over for all our migratory birds. Social barriers have relaxed, too. Conglomerate groups of robins and flickers, bluebirds and sparrows assemble in our mowings or ramble through our locusts, more for companionship, I think, than with any immediate intention of travel. On the bare peak of our tallest hill, where the wind blows free, barnswallows are training their young for a South American cruise.

I sit with my dogs in the afternoon and watch the flying school. Fleet blue and chestnut bodies scribble arabesques upon the sky. They dive and soar, glide and swing with soft twitterings and the glitter of perfect wings. I can tell the elders from the novices only when, with a miraculous fluttering pause in midair, a parent thrusts captured insects into a child's mouth and then flies on. The small, shining shapes, their grace and freedom of movement lift my heart. It is commentary on the purposes and ends of man that, with the swallows' loveliness and liberty close at hand, he ignores these and chooses the lumbering and rapacious eagle for his national emblem.

Heat still endures through the days, but the nights grow cool. Althea and I no longer need to mitigate our own discomfort on sultry evenings by deploring the probable distress of folk immured in cities. We need extra wraps now when we sit on our platform and watch night's tide flow up the valley. If the songs of birds no longer brighten twilight, it rings with the small clamor of insect voices frantically shouting of love before the first frost falls.

Though much of Frederick's days of labor and a good deal of my own spare time is occupied in defending our farm against their depredations, I find myself, when the shrill din of little voices raises itself at nightfall, rather envying insects. Theirs is a more logical and a happier existence than our own. Death, for them, comes at life's peak and not, as with man, somewhere along the further, downward slope. Theirs is the better drama. Theirs, I suspect, is the more enviable way.

The time of the insect's labor is his extreme youth. As a grub, he works nonunion hours, painfully groping along or through earth, breadwinning, toiling, spinning at last the cocoon from which a winged and amorous avatar at last bursts free. Insects know in old age joys that mankind must segregate in his own earlier years. Senescence for the butterfly means gay raiment, blithe flight, persistent patronage of innumerable floral cabarets and culminating passion before the frost comes down. The elderly cricket fiddles away his last days in cheery defiance of the imminent, bleak morrow. I hear him now when I wake at night.

Sometimes, more fortunately, he is in the dew-drenched grass below my window. At that distance his music is soothing. Sometimes, I discover he has got into my bedroom and it presently is borne in upon me as his strident sawing continues that one or the other of us must leave if I am to have any more slumber, for a bull cricket going great guns close at hand is no more soothing than a snoring roommate.

The speedy capture of my unwelcome serenader is a project requiring specialized equipment, a deal of resourcefulness and a deftly compliant body. I arm myself with a flashlight and attempt to track him down in orthodox stalking posture, body close to earth, face scraping the floor, for it is cricket habit to lair as far as possible under the room's lowest furnishing.

The cricket, too, is nature's most eminent ventriloquist as anyone who has tried to find the source of his music at two o'clock in the morning soon discovers. Usually, while peering under bureaus, chests and radiators, I discover a number of items that Althea and I thought we had lost before I finally come face to face with the small, dark musician.

Thereafter, if I am deft and he is not, I enclose him quickly in a hand and drop him from the window. More often, the stalking is only the preliminary to a strenuous and disheveling chase. Frequently, the thumping sounds I make and my accompanying language rouse Althea. I have gathered from what she has said at such times that her sympathies are more with the cricket than with her predatory spouse. We talk about that, too, at some length before we go to sleep again.

Human beings themselves proclaim by their conduct the approach of autumn. In a little while now, the falling leaves will disclose to us, the fortunate who live here all year, the rough lines of ridges, the cliffs and ledges and hollows—all the stark, essential features of the land that summer has hidden. In a little while, the summer people will have departed and the normal life of our community, concealed since June by a horde of sojourners, will resume its ordained place in our lives.

Meanwhile, the imported and superimposed social life of the region quickens its tempo as August wanes. Gestures must be made, hospitality must be requited before the summer people leave us. The Blanks who have dined with us must discharge that obligation along with more formal debits to tradesmen. Sundry folk who have been here for cocktail parties must pay us back. I find myself waking with sensations in my mouth and head far more reminiscent of Manhattan than Windham County, Vermont. I find myself, too, beginning to look forward to September's hegira.

Life may or may not be more pleasant after the vacationists leave. At least, it will be more natural. We shall recover in a few weeks now the slow rhythm we have learned to love since we came to dwell in Vermont. When that departs; when, as is entirely possible, this region becomes another "vacationland," with most of its property owned by part-time residents and most of its native stock gone from the prim, white farmhouses, something sustaining and essential will have evaporated from the lives of Althea and me for which the presence of even the most delightful outlanders will not entirely compensate. This, I am aware, is class treason, but we can't help it.

We are resolute liberals, Althea and I. Some of our best friends are summer people. We feel toward the temporary sojourner here no more arrogance than the veteran with five campaign ribbons displays toward the R.O.T.C. rookie. Folk may have summered in Vermont for twenty years, they may have wealth and culture far surpassing ours as well as fame that we never shall attain, but that doesn't disquiet us. We have lived here for six whole winters. We consider that record and smile condescendingly.

It is well, I suppose, that vacationists should bring a metropolitan flavor into our lives. If it serves no other purpose, it keeps us from ever wishing to go back and live in New York again. We conform to the courteous example set by our neighbors and welcome each year the return of summer people. We may diverge from the norm by welcoming their departure, too, though I doubt it. Summer people have their uses. While they are here, they at least let Althea and me feel superior to someone. For the rest of the year, we occupy the lowest grade in the local caste system.

This is a matter worthy of more study than ever we have found time to give it. It may seem perverse that a state implicitly and explicitly democratic should cherish so rigid a class consciousness. It is neither offensive nor ostentatious. It simply exists, intricately braided with the still, intense state pride that is Vermonters' most universal passion. You can win even more applause from an audience here by praising the commonwealth's integrity and dignity than you can by lambasting the Democratic Party.

As a matter of fact, Vermonters in general regard Democrats who dwell among them with the same broad tolerance the state displays toward the eccentricities of summer folk. Here, men may live in error if they please and seldom is anything done to bring them into salvation. I do know of one elderly Green Mountaineer who, while visiting his daughter in another state, trumpeted so loudly of the glories of the Republican party that one of his auditors at last asked:

"Mr. Smith, aren't there any Democrats at all in your home town?"

"There was one," the other replied after thought. "A while ago."

"And what became of him?"

"Wal, finally the better folks in town got together and made him behave himself."

Vermont's attitude of reservation toward new settlers is rooted, I imagine, in nothing more dubious than native caution. Men who are reluctant to buy a cow without full knowledge of her qualities and ancestry look equivocally upon outlanders whose backgrounds and records, before they came, necessarily are obscure. It follows that Vermonters esteem their fellow natives most highly because they know them best. Peter himself keeps no more thorough a tabulation of the sins and virtues of mortals than the average Yankee cherishes of his neighbors'.

Next in order of merit to the purebred Green Mountaineer come other folk of clean New England stock. These can be accepted more heartily than other foreigners for the sake of their upbringing, but they do not win complete confidence however admirable may be their lives. I know of at least two men who, though they have won political preferment in the state, have found the fact that they were born in Massachusetts no small handicap.

Below Vermonters and New Englanders in general come persons from elsewhere who live and vote here. Their popularity varies according to their works, but they all are lumped together under the heading, City Folks. Althea and I belong to that caste. Our humble state might gall us, if we were not able to look down from this lowly height upon, Summer People.

We feel toward these the particularly delightful intolerance that is the perquisite of the recently emancipated. Althea and I once were Summer People ourselves.

The part-time residents can be broken up into several distinct groups. Natives do not seem to make the effort, but Althea and I have classified at least three species— Round Pegs, Square Pegs and Missionaries—on a descending scale.

The Round Pegs are those whom, each spring, we are happiest to see return; whom we most nearly miss when they leave in September. No fanfare accompanies their entrances and exits. They come unobtrusively back to old houses that they have restored. These are only summer residences now, but they are planned to be permanent homes in their owners' declining years.

Their dooryards are adorned with the shrubs and the small, unostentatious gardens of the region. Their rooms are furnished more wholly in the New England tradition than those of their native neighbors. The Round Pegs are here because they have found a way of life that they love. They walk as decorously, they mind their own business as completely as the Vermonters do themselves. They are passionately addicted to auctions and eager attendants at strawberry festivals and corn roasts. Neither reforming zeal nor patronage accompanies them. They fit nicely into the background they have chosen with no disarrangement of the scenery and, in a little while, they and the natives are hailing each other by their first names.

The Square Pegs bring their backgrounds along with them, complete with appropriate customs and costumes from Greenwich Village or Park Avenue and set them down upon a mildly amazed countryside. If they be wealthy, they transform inoffensive farmhouses into mansions or monstrosities or both. If they are pressed for funds and have come to this region to retrench and save money, they gird long and loud over the penny-pinching qualities of the Yankee.

The Square Pegs' and Althea's and my impressions of life in Vermont vary radically, possibly because they survey it only through perpetual, if imperceptible, lorgnettes. Imported servants sometimes accompany the Square Pegs. They have found by trial and error that Vermonters do not take kindly to the uniforms and postures of well-drilled menials. If they be querulous, the Square Pegs compile long lists of grievances against the native character and will recite these at length on the least encouragement. If they be more philosophical, they consider the local peasantry quaint and very, very entertaining.

The Square Pegs disregard local custom and tradition. They also, not infrequently, overthrow a sturdy old literary standard that has flourished since before the birth of the republic. It has a stencil quality that should be familiar to every reader.

City people always are victimized by rapacious Yankees —in books. Guileless and open-handed urbanites are the traditional dupes of penny-pinching, bargain-driving New Englanders—in novels. There is another side to the picture. Here, we look most often upon that reverse.

Natives whom I know, in their dealings with summer folk, more often are the defrauded than the fraudulent. Contrary to tradition, the average Vermonter is trustworthy and trustful. He extends elastic credit to his neighbors and, too often, to strangers. My own intelligence system still is elemental, but I have compiled an impressive roster of Square Pegs who are remembered most vividly in our town for the debts they left behind them.

I can't tell what the average Vermonter thinks of the Square Peg, rattling about so dissonantly in his round hole. I never have heard the opinion uttered. The native accords this species, as a rule, the particularly blighting criticism of no comment at all and, though Square Pegs may have been coming to Vermont for twenty years, they still remain rigidly "Mr. and Mrs. Blank" to a whole neighborhood, which is a fairly complete biography in itself.

There have been times when Althea and I have suspected, for all the Square Pegs' resolute observance of the forms and ceremonies of urban social conduct; for all their luncheons and the like to the acceptable of our summer world, that actually they are lonely. Otherwise they would not descend upon former Manhattanites with such overwhelming warmth. It may be just innate cordiality. To me it more resembles the rapture of castaways who see in a wilderness a face from home. The Square Pegs tell us that they come to Vermont for rest and seclusion. They get it.

Less endurable to folk in the pleasant process of going native are aspirations and attempted conversions by the Missionaries. These summer people are difficult and dedicated folk who insist on myopically regarding the self-sufficient Yankee as a benighted and shut-in person sorely in need of inspirational assistance.

One would bring alleviation and cheer to our meager lives by embroiling local farmers in the art of eurythmics. Another would bestow the blessing of self-expression upon us by initiating a Little Theater movement, overlooking blandly the Vermonter's truly monumental gift for self-expression when faced with the prospect of appearing in even a P.T.A. playlet.

There are plans for all sorts of improvements to our lot, ranging from glee clubs to co-operative slaughter houses, advanced each summer by starry-eyed enthusiasts and perishing in a heavy miasma of local indifference every fall.

The Missionaries are the well-intentioned, if maddening, folk who cannot leave things alone. They consider Vermont a peculiarly backward province of the Appalachian wilderness. Their benevolence is not only a little presumptuous but purblind as well. In striving to reorder the Green Mountain way of life, they overlook the fact that the native here leads, more nearly than any other breed I know, the sort of life that suits him best. He has his own fun in his own way and, to a bystander like me, it seems better and saner amusement than any of the substitutes poked at him by the Missionaries.

The Vermonter is too busy in summer taking care of his farm and of helpless summer people to have much time for folly. Native social life goes to earth and stays there pretty thoroughly during the vacation season. I wish the Missionaries who try to supply my neighbors with unsought recreation could glimpse the rich variety in which this is offered during the supposedly privation-filled winter months.

They will be leaving us soon now—the Round Pegs, the Square Pegs and the Missionaries, each after his own tribe. Constellations of wild carrot blossoms shine in the firmament of our mowings. Along the ridges of the hills, tree tops grow faintly tarnished with autumn's first and tentative hues. Each night, sometime between the clear cool hour of our going to bed and our waking, fog rises and steeps the world so that every morning wears a moonstone hue.

Fall is close at hand. Frost will soon be upon us. This is the time when produce for the final canning session is brought in and Black Boy's unwilling vigil in the mid-garden dog coop is almost ended. This is the time shades are pulled down and shutters are closed in almost half our town's dwellings. This is the time when the summer people go home again and life resumes its calm, beloved normality for Althea and me.

# CHAPTER NINE

# September

ALTHEA AND I, since we came to live in the country, have wondered increasingly over mankind's disparagement of September. No month, save possibly February, receives so little notice or esteem. August is the time of summer's flood tide, the traditional season for human holiday. October's splendor inspires, yearly, innumerable pages of verse which, if laid end to end, might better be left that way. Intervening September is neglected, an undistinguished valley between two peaks of annual experience. It is irresolute, transitional, holding fast to summer's peace and yet leading perceptibly toward fall.

That is man's opinion. That, Althea and I remember, was our own impression of September before we moved to Vermont. It was, to us, a sad time, when adults went back to cities from vacations and children returned wretchedly to school. We know otherwise. Each year increases our conviction. Actually, September is not a humble season at all. It has not—as once I believed, since it is my birth month—the climatic duplication of my own mentality, inclining in one direction momentarily, only to swing toward the other on the morrow; unstable, deplorable.

September, Althea and I know now, is a period of upheaval and violence. It is the most revolutionary of months. In our quiet lives, it furnishes that faint flavor of danger without which no delight can be wholly savored. Things happen to us and to all Vermont in September— meteorological and more animate things.

Sometimes the weather supplies nothing more violent than the "line storm," the cold protracted downpour that local wisdom says, and science denies, accompanies the autumnal equinox. This cuts fresh gullies in our long-suffering road—usually just after the local authorities have at last got round to mending it. The storm beats down our flowers and does its creditable best to wipe away all traces of summer that water can absolve. Last year, instead of a mere line storm, we had a hurricane.

Though we have concealed the fact from the public until now, it was Althea and I who evoked the rain loaded blast that tore our countryside apart. On September 21st, 1938, we drove our son to his school.

During the years of his sojourn, each trip we made thither was accompanied by violent aberrations of the weather. In fall, it always rained; in winter, we brought down sleet storms or blizzards; in spring, we roused the rivers to flood. When we took our son back to school for his final year of secondary education, we outstripped all our earlier considerable accomplishments. That time, the hurricane accompanied us homeward and we and the tempest arrived at Dummerston, hand in hand.

More accurately, Althea did not get home at all and I reached our dwelling only after a three-mile walk, a deal

of wading and an excessive amount of climbing over prostrate trees. For once, our carrier pigeon passion to return
to our own place was blocked, in part, but it took a major
upheaval of nature to thwart that imperative desire which
obsesses Althea and me when we are homeward bound.

We tried our best, that afternoon of tempest. We are
accustomed to opposition in our homecomings. We attempted all the possible ways leading to our farm. Along
each of these, we drove valiantly upstream against waxing
torrents of brown water. When we reached the inevitable
barrier of uprooted trees, we turned around and tried
another thoroughfare.

Meanwhile, the squealing wind hurried in precocious
dusk. Incredible bursts of rain smacked upon our car's
windshield and, in the dim woods on either hand, tall
pines and maples let go their rootholds on drenched earth
and wearily went down.

We were not specially frightened. The thing had not
burst upon us. It had been growing gradually all day long
and when the hour of climax came and the storm shoul-
dered the car, as though determined to overset it, and
foaming streams replaced familiar roads and the wind's
voice rose to a vicious screech, these things found us partly
conditioned. It was only afterward that we were terrified
by thought of all that might have happened—and did not.

At the time, Althea and I were concerned chiefly with
getting home. This and the odd tumult occupied our
minds. We never had heard a gale cry out in quite so
strange a key. It reminded us, we told each other, of
the sound track accompanying a moving picture storm

sequence. Thus far had current life removed us from actuality and thus far, for once, Hollywood was accurate.

Finally, we found ourselves trapped. A stand of overset locust trees lay across the road before us, like gigantic mown weeds, and when we tried to turn about, we found that other trees had fallen behind.

"We'll have to walk," Althea said.

"It'll be dangerous," I told her.

"Goodness," she answered, "if nothing has hit our car, there's much less chance of anything falling on just you and me. We've got to get home. Think of poor Bertha."

Bertha was then our brand-new cook, successor to Ruth who had found life in our household so monotonously tranquil that she had left us to wed for a third time. Bertha, a lady of monumental calm, had been promised when we had departed that morning that we would return early. She was alone in an unfamiliar house—if the house still were there—with no companionship at hand save the dubious society of three strange dogs.

I didn't argue with Althea. In moments of stress she is not to be diverted from her purpose. We left our car in a farmer's barnyard and started our march. It was not an easy advance, for the wind pushed us and rain stung, but we plodded on through thickening gloom, ducking past bent and quivering upright trees, scrambling over the fallen. By the time we reached Hazel's house, a mile further on our way, this undulatory progress had exhausted Althea. I left her there with the hope that she and her hostess's dwelling both would be present on my return, borrowed a torch and went on.

It took me two hours to accomplish the remaining three miles to our home. The wind was failing, but it still rained hard and thrice, following the main road, I had to wade through impressive brooks, foaming along where no proper watercourse had any business. It had grown dark too. I did not appreciate the depth of the gloom until after I had fallen and broken the torch. Thereafter, I advanced by the touch system.

Our driveway was a long barricade of overthrown trees. Cold panic, that gripped me as I struggled through them, did not expedite progress. If here in the hollow there was so inordinate an amount of wreckage, how much of our house could possibly be left on the hill above?

I have never confessed, even to Althea, how abjectly frightened I became as unseen branches slapped my face, hooked themselves into my clothing and, reaching downward, maliciously tripped me. I am ashamed of it now, yet I still think my terror pardonable. Althea has wondered sometimes whether either of us really knows how much we love our home. I know I spanned and plumbed the depths of my own passion as I floundered toward what might no longer be a dwelling but a disjointed lumber pile.

And then, at last, I was through the blasted woodland and the uphill stretch of road glimmered, unobstructed, in the blackness before me. I ran, less with any thought of belated rescue than to be rid as soon as possible of unendurable doubt, and paused, thoroughly blown, at the turn from which one gains his first glimpse of our house and its shielding cluster of locust trees.

They were there still, a blacker mass against a dark sky, but the outline of the grove had changed. When I was able to move forward again, I found that many of the trees had been uprooted. The top of the biggest was thrust into our doorway. I had to tear my way through it. I could see no light and all I could hear was the pelting rain and the hooting wind. Then, as I reached the door, my dogs gave tongue and I, opening the portal, marked the glimmer of faint radiance in the kitchen.

There I found the storm tossed remnant of our household. By the light of one candle, Bertha sat at the table. The power line had blown away hours before. Pressed close against her and still cowering from the sound and the fury they had endured were our three dogs.

"Well!" Bertha said.

Her Bible lay open on the table before her. While the hurricane had raged and five locusts had crashed down about the house, she had sat thus for hours, reading the Word and waiting for the roof to blow off. My dogs now surrendered to canine hysterics. I waited for a more painful human version. Bertha closed her Bible and got up.

"Well," she said again, "I'm real glad you've come."

Fortitude, in Vermont, is the first of the cardinal virtues.

I have no clear memory of the walk back to where Althea and I spent the night or of what I ate for supper or of how at last I got to bed, but I recall the morrow's sunrise. Another September is here now and I think often of that night and the following daybreak and find therein an augury while the course of another hurricane moves westward.

I rose at dawn. It was the quiet that wakened me. I looked from my window. The air was warm and fragrant with the scents of freshly splintered wood, bruised leaves, and soaked earth. All about lay the wreckage of spent and senseless fury—torn soil, abased treetops and the crookedly clutching gestures of broken roots. The east was clear yellow. I waited by the window until sunlight came over the New Hampshire hills. Then I heard on the washed and blocked road the snort of a truck, the thump of axes, a shovel's clinking and I knew the purposeless disaster was over and that men, the plain men of our town, already were repairing the vast disorder of a stricken world.

In the year that has passed since last September's hurricane, many of its wounds have been hidden. We have replaced the old barn roof which was removed practically entire and have been taught still another painful lesson in the vanity of amateur farming. The urge to wrest profit from our acres is our ever-present temptation. The mathematics of our attempt to make money out of our hay last year may restrain us from further like ventures.

Why, Althea and I asked each other, a year ago last June, should we try to sell our hay standing at what must obviously be a considerable loss to ourselves? Why should we not harvest it, since we still had a barn that stubbornly refused to fall down, and sell it, piecemeal, along toward spring when hay was scarce and high in price? Satan, standing at our elbows, decreed that we should be deaf to these questions' obvious answers.

It cost us $75 to cut and store the best of our hay. The rest we burned standing. We should have been wiser if we had burned the barn too. When the hurricane tore away its roof, something had to be done at once, lest our investment be wholly destroyed by subsequent rain. So, instead of wisely letting the elements pull the rest of the structure apart, we spent $140 on a roof. Thereafter, our senile barn wore a rakish and implausible appearance. It looked, Althea said, like a tramp crowned by a new silk hat.

We comforted ourselves with the thought that, if we sold all our hay for a good price in spring, we should be less than $50 out on the enterprise. We did not sell a single ton. The hay still molders in our barn and if ever we wish to have it cleared out, we shall have to pay someone to do it.

All in all, our attempt to make money from our hay has cost us some $215. There are, Althea and I believe, pleasanter ways of spending that amount. We tell each other that you can't wring profit from a farm unless you are by birth and training a farmer. We hope we will continue to remember that truth, but we suspect that, in the face of another like temptation, we shan't.

The hurricane robbed us not only of our barn roof, the tool house door, several patches of shingles from the house itself and innumerable trees, but Harry our original hired man also was blown away in its aftermath, though it was I and no celestial power who supplied the blast.

I do not know when or how discontent first was planted in our hired man's bosom. My knowledge of essential

Vermont nature is too slight for me to be sure. It may have been that Harry felt our installation of an electric fence about the garden was implicit criticism of his own system of deer resistance. It may have been that he regarded the small cottage we built for his use as a presumptuous attempt to wean him from his own way of life.

Whatever the cause, Althea and I had been aware all summer that dissonance was creeping into the quiet harmony of our lives and that Harry was supplying it. So dependent upon him had we become that we were stricken when Harry first spoke darkly of "making a change." As the weeks passed, we were able to view that prospect more philosophically.

Harry was away on Wednesday when the hurricane smote us. Harry returned, with none of the look of one who had been blown into a far country, on Saturday. By then, I had been hacking debris out of our road for two days and slowly filling with the peculiarly corrosive grievance against any available object that enforced physical labor always supplies. It was a relief to see Harry. It was an additional comfort to speak to him before breakfast when the pentecostal flame burns almost visibly upon my forehead.

Harry accepted dismissal with true Vermont impassiveness. Once the deed was done, Althea and I were more perceptibly grieved than he. He left that night. He explained, with logical Vermont thrift, that since he already had been working for an hour when I saw him, it would be better for him to finish the day.

No visible marks of sorrow attended his departure. If

[ 157 ]

he cherished reluctance to go, I suspect that it was purely literary. He may have felt that the reading public was being brusquely deprived of a favorite character.

I don't know. Althea and I, since then, sometimes have wondered whether, for all our long intimacy, for all the communal enterprises in which we were engaged, actually we ever really knew Harry at all.

This September promises milder violences than the last. Summer, which has passed with what seems to Althea and me such indecent haste, grants us now a series of serenely brilliant days, as one in his old age makes bequests and orders his life so that, when it is spent, men may remember him fondly.

Mornings and evenings have an odd, clear light. The air itself is inherently brilliant. It intensifies the sunlight, stresses shadows so clearly that hills no longer are green, tilted barriers but sharply limned masses of individual trees. Nights are cool and the dampness they lay upon the woods quickens mushrooms and fungi, each according to its tribe. These raise small pale umbrellas by the paths and the red russulae spread in the shade imitation pools of slaughter.

No frost has touched us yet, but overtones of alien color already lie upon the treetops and in our pasture one impetuous maple blazes. The peace and the beauty of the summer still dwell here, but Althea and I know that beneath bright tranquillity the tide has turned and moves in upon us again.

Life has flowed outward from our home all summer. Now, imperceptibly, the six months' beleaguerment of our dwelling and of us begins. We must prepare for siege, fortify and garrison our house against animate and inanimate invaders.

Mice who have taken their vacation at large are coming in from the fields. We have first notice of their presence by delicate flutterings in our walls and by sudden outbursts of violence, evenings in the living room—wild barkings, runnings to and fro, overturned furniture and a general hurly-burly that ends only when the temeritous mouse has escaped or else has been extinguished by one or the other of three dogs, each of whom will claim credit for the deed.

Dougal and Meg are adept in catching mice, but Black Boy has qualities in this regard that the Scottish terriers lack. Althea has looked upon the Newfoundland with horror-tinctured awe ever since that morning when she and Dougal argued about the removal of a dead mouse from the kitchen. It was Dougal's property, but he was stubborn about carrying it outside. He pretended to misunderstand Althea's ever more vehement commands. The mouse still lay on the linoleum when Black Boy ambled in, beamed upon the contestants, bent over the subject of strife, inhaled briefly, gulped and proceeded on his way, having settled the argument beyond any hope of revival.

Rats who pestered us sorely two winters ago will be returning to our cellar now, to raid our storeroom and ignore our most artfully set traps. In time, even Bertha may come to mourn the untimely demise of our snake.

He lived unhonored and he died unsung, but he did keep our basement very satisfactorily clear of pests. For more than a year he occupied a place like that of the debauchee in an otherwise respectable family. Everyone was aware of him, but no one gave him public mention.

Our snake was known to us by his works before we ever saw him. We grew aware that the rat population in our cellar, which had taken up residence there when a weasel had come to live in our barn, inexplicably was decreasing in number and depredations. There was less scurrying and squealing at night. Presently, no more jars of preserves were knocked off the storeroom shelves to shatter on the concrete floor and serve as provender for our unwelcome tenants. Since the dozen traps we had set remained unsprung, I could not understand the abatement of the plague until I came suddenly one day upon its author.

He was a checkered adder, large of girth and harmless despite his sinister name. He was coiled in a corner by the cellar stairs. I had the sense of shock, the sharp constriction of the stomach, unexpected encounter with one of his tribe always inflicts and my first thought was to look about me for a weapon. Then, since he showed no fear but lay quietly watching me, felonious assault seemed a sorry greeting for even an uninvited guest. I went my way and said nothing, only praying that Ruth, our then cook, never would see him. Hers was an effervescent temperament and her dread of snakes was mortal. Meanwhile, rats continued to diminish and finally to vanish and the mice, the beetles and the occasional frogs that had made progress through our cellar precarious disappeared also.

Ruth never laid eyes on our snake. He was not an obtrusive character though I wished, when he shed his skin, that he had hung his castoff raiment in a corner. Instead, he left it in the middle of the cellar floor and Ruth came upon it and uttered ear-piercing alarums. These continued long after she had returned in disheveled haste to the kitchen.

"Down there. A snake skin. Right out on the floor. Glory be, I wouldn't go down again for a fortune till someone's taken that awful thing out."

So I went downstairs and carried the snake's discarded winter suit past the shuddering Ruth and outdoors. That satisfied her completely. No linking of cause and effect led her to postulate that, where the snakeskin had been, an actual snake, in all probability, still must be. Ruth had the fortunate and myopic mind that never looks far toward trouble.

It was months before Bertha, Ruth's successor, saw our cellar resident. She took no pleasure in the meeting, but on being assured that he was one of the family, she accepted him with the philosophy all our employees have displayed toward Althea's and my soft hearted aberrations. They cannot understand our desire to share our farm with tenants of long standing, but they humor us. Our hired man, early this summer, sent me an urgent message.

"Frederick wants to know whether the hawk in the butternut tree is a personal friend of yours or can he shoot it?"

The redtail who nests each summer in our woods is a very warm personal friend and Frederick did not shoot it.

Wherefore, Bertha endured our snake's unobtrusive presence. She quaked majestically whenever she descended to the cellar and at length her valor had its reward. Not until I saw her glee at our boarder's demise, did I appreciate how much she had dreaded him.

Bertha, a few weeks ago, led me with muted paeans of triumph into our basement. The snake lay dead, caught in a forgotten trap that long ago we had set for the very rats he had abolished. There was a saturnine poetic justice in his end and though Bertha is delighted and even Althea secretly is relieved, the time is at hand when I think they both will regret his passing.

The invasion by small creatures, who already are aware that soon our house will be sole oasis of warmth in a snow desert, is only one evidence that winter is just over the horizon.

Nights now have a foreboding chill and, no matter how hot the day may have been, stars burn with new vehemence and each morning finds grass and brush bowed down by weight of dew.

Althea and I tend our flowers with that special affection bestowed on those doomed to untimely deaths. We inspect the thermometer each night before bedtime and wonder whether the end will come before sunrise. We have lived long enough in this region to have acquired at least a portion of the countryside's pagan attitude. Wherefore, beside consulting the thermometer, we match its testimony with the phases of the moon.

## September

The first frost, so local lore holds, will not fall while September's moon is waning. If the full passes without this disaster, our gardens will be safe until the new moon appears.

Such superstitions and dubious foretellings are, I imagine, inevitable by-products in all agricultural life. Realistic Vermont is not proof against them. They flourish here. They are recited with jesting surface skepticism, but they are an actual part of our existence and their roots run back into no man knows what dark anthropological jungles.

By auguries and inherited aphorisms, those who depend on the whims of soil and weather for livelihood keep at arms' length acknowledgments of their own impotence. Sense of utter subservience is unendurable to man. He evades this by clinging to quaint, empirical doctrines that, whatever else their value, afford him a feeling of power and divination.

Most of our myths are involved with the weather itself. Some may easily be trailed back to Sumer and Memphis. Others are more inscrutable.

A ring around the moon predicts a storm. The number of stars within that ring foretells how many days will pass before the storm breaks.

The date of the first snow represents the number of snowfalls we shall have that winter.

The weather on each of the twelve days after Christmas—warm or cold, clear or stormy—establishes the general climatic conditions for each of the twelve subsequent months.

The shape of a hog's spleen at November butchering time foretells to the rural augur the severity of the coming winter.

When fir trees are heavily coned, one may expect an open winter.

If robins return in March, that means a late and stormy spring.

Brush cut in the dark of the moon will not grow again.

When cornhusks are thick or beechnuts heavy, there is prospect of a hard winter.

If yellow jackets build their nests high, snows will be deep.

Crops should not be planted when the moon is waning.

Rheumatic pain can be relieved by wearing a horse chestnut over its site.

Pears can be kept from splitting by driving a nail into the trunk of the tree.

These are samples. There are many more and Althea and I have learned to bring them forth on occasion with an expert air. Their frequently demonstrated fraudulence makes no difference. Lore like this does no harm and it gives to agricultural people a sense of authority over implacable powers.

By the signs that are spread about us, we may not be able to read accurately what winter will be, but innumerable portents tell of its approach and each day of warmth and brilliance has become a gift greatly to be cherished.

The katydid that appears inexplicably each September on our living room wall has made his sixth annual entrance. He is autumn's green, mute herald.

Occasionally, I find one of his fellows in our fields. Each to an unscientific eye seems normal, but none of them chants his rasping, persistent accusation. They are dumb in this region, though fifteen miles down the valley they sing all night.

I do not deplore their restrain, for the insistent voice of the katydid in my youth was proclamation that holidays almost were over and the schooling of another year was about to begin. The sound still brings a heaviness to my heart.

The air is weighted with a feeling of change. We sense it when we work in our perennial garden where asters are lavender, white and blue and the first chrysanthemums blossom. It oppresses me when I go walking with my dogs. All nine of them, three adults and six puppies, move through the brittle grass in a glittering spray of grasshoppers. To these, the elders pay no heed, but the agile things are big game to a half-dozen small black blunderers whose progress still is whimsical but whose hearts are high. The puppies stalk and pounce and occasionally catch and swallow a victim. I can tell how many have been fortunate in the hunt by the number who are profusely sick afterward.

Meggy's children themselves are eloquent prophets of imminent change. We can't possibly keep nine dogs. Althea says so, but she is something less than helpful in her inability to choose certainly which one we shall retain. It must, we have told each other, be the best of the litter. We agree on that loudly and continue to foster heresies in our own hearts. The trouble with our three grown dogs has been that we have esteemed personality above show points. Five of our pups must leave us soon.

For this and other reasons, we find ourselves intensely, almost desperately, holding fast to each day of the receding summer. We revel in sights and sounds and scents that, we know, soon will be gone.

It may be that Stevenson in his *Suicide Club* uttered a greater truth than he knew. Sense of impermanence is needed to bring out the full flavor of life. Existence is sweeter because, inevitably, winter must come.

*CHAPTER TEN*

# October

ON THREE successive weekends this October, Althea and I assured the friends who came to receive their long-promised puppies that now the autumn foliage was at its peak of splendor. Each time, we believed it ourselves.

The fourth and final car has borne away the last of Meg's litter whom we can bear to let go and, with the anguish of quadruple partings at an end, we wonder why after five autumns here we still are unable to be sure when the hills actually burn brightest.

They are more sober now. The oaks' dull reds, the aspens' tardy yellow weave with the firs' dark green a Persian pattern and bared branches, intermingling, hold a smoky, bluish hue. This, Althea and I tell each other, lacking further audience, is indeed the pageant's climax.

We have watched its progress with an infatuation that folk supposedly as busy as we should accord to nothing but their tasks. We have refrained with what we like to think is Spartan fortitude from driving to Dover, Wardsboro and Wilmington to see how their shows compare with our own. The parade of color that has passed our small reviewing stand has been all two pairs of eyes adequately could heed. Perhaps, another year, we shall remember its sequence and be less headlong in hailing any particular day as the spectacle's summit.

We have seen the birches turn to gold and, coin by coin, pay earth a year's ground rent, and beeches blaze and tarnish, and, before their hue has left the slopes, have watched soft maples become pillars of still fire. Tall sugar maples have added their endless variations of yellow and orange. Then has come a pause and we have believed the display has ended and have been abashed as oaks have flamed and reluctant aspens suddenly have changed into clouds of sparkling sequins above pale trunks.

We have sat, longer hours than we dare confess but a much shorter space than we wish we might have spent, far up our hill on still, bright afternoons to scan the red ranges and the tapestried valleys. We have pointed out incredibilities of light and shade and color, vehemently, as though the speaker presumed his mate were dim of sight and wit; or we have waited, saying nothing, while small birds scuffled in the brush and jays called from hill to hill and spent leaves let go in the crystalline silence and fell to earth with the faintest, fragile clattering.

And now frost has come, to blacken our vegetable patch and wilt our cutting garden. In our perennial bed, asters and phlox have succumbed. Only a few clumps of chrysanthemums still lift their heads. Frederick, who usually is impervious to heat or cold, chops wood each night to temper the morning atmosphere of his cottage. No longer may Althea and I steal our own time. Winter approaches and there are two heathen puppies to instruct in household decorum before the nights grow so chill that they must desert their kennel and be brought indoors as respectable members of the family.

We have five dogs now, Dougal, Meg and Black Boy and our pick of the puppies whom Althea has named Wullie and Cricket. These last are our substitutes for him whom we had intended to choose solely for his symmetry and show points. These are what we selected instead of the physical paragon that we highly had resolved to raise as a balance for our other dogs' structural deficiencies. In the five months since their birth, Althea and I have weighed and judged and debated so that we might choose for our own the most nearly physically perfect pup. Wullie and Cricket are what we got.

The twin brother and sister are five months old today. No formal festivities have marked the event. None have been needed. To the puppies, each successive morning is a new celebration. Wullie, who esteems consistency above morality, once more has dug out the oft-refilled hole among the foundation's evergreens. He lies in the excavation now, a philosophical sinner who deems iniquity worth its punishment. Cricket, with hue and cry, again has attempted suicide beneath an approaching car that stopped abruptly and just in time. Temporarily, she is completely crushed by Althea's scolding. Her penitence will endure until the next automobile ascends our hill.

Life at the moment is as tranquil as it can be in any place where four Scottish terriers and a Newfoundland pursue their several ways and I, looking from my window out upon the richly colored hills and down upon the abject Cricket and the laired, insurgent Wullie, think of the perfect pup we might have had and have not and am momentarily grateful that the more important problems of the world are not in the hands of soft-headed sentimentalists like Althea and me. In the light of what has happened, our debates and disagreements over the comparative physical excellences of our six pups seem faintly pathetic.

We watched the progress of Meg's children with such high hopes. We were sure that no litter that had five champions among their more immediate ancestors could fail to produce at least one perfect specimen. It may be that the paragon was not among the animate black capsules who paddled themselves with much shrill complaint about the whelping box on disproportionate bellies; who rose at last on unsteady legs and walked drunkenly; who developed a propensity for shrill and continual hell-raising that endeared them to me and disgusted their mother; who dwelt most of the summer and early fall in an outdoor pen and filled it with spontaneous riot and equally unpremeditated slumber. It may be that, actually, there was no perfect pup in that disreputable sextet. I am certain only of this: If he were there, Althea and I did not keep him.

Yet, we did make our choice by a process of elimination. We identified the more flagrant failures and discarded from strength. The runtish female with the apologetic air clearly was not for us. The smallest male, too, was doomed to rejection. He had cow hocks and also a crook in his tail, uncannily resembling the defect of Dougal, who positively was not his accredited sire.

I cannot tell where the puppy acquired this misfortune. The tails of his registered parents are impeccably straight and stubby, but I do know that when I discussed the odd coincidence with Althea, Dougal looked at nothing with a faraway expression and I thought I heard him hum a little, sentimental air.

The tail of the pup who became in time our leading candidate was satisfactorily brief. He was a sturdy young hellion with an immense energy and no chemical trace of reverence—earliest out of the kennel in the morning, last to enter at night, a swaggering, slightly raffish young man who first called himself to Althea's attention by biting her shrewdly in the ankle.

He would, Althea said grimly as she retired to change a torn stocking, need a deal of disciplining and, as far as she was concerned, it couldn't begin too soon.

The leading candidate, it seemed to us, had a character somewhat less admirable than his physique. He wasted less admiration upon us than his brothers and sisters spent. He reserved most of that quality for his own person. I think he sneered at the gay affection Crooktail lavished on all mortals. He would, as Althea had said, need much corrective education, but he had points and they, after all, were the purpose of our enterprise.

These grew more obvious as time went on—a well-boned head, small ears, stubby tail, thick body and sturdy legs. No other in the litter was so excellently made, though save for Crooktail, the cowhocked, they all were good puppies. In late September, Althea and I made what we told each other was the final and decisive inspection.

"This is the best dog," I told her, holding the paragon, who snarled falsetto and struggled.

"All right," Althea said with no expression of voice or visage, "then we better get rid of the others as quickly as ever we can."

Her counsel was wise. Six pups were too many even for me to wish to keep and the longer we cherished them, the sorer we knew would be the anguish of parting. Besides, I had promised Althea that we should retain only one and had issued promissory notes, payable on presentation, for one puppy to our worthiest dog-loving friends.

It seemed to us that the pup we had selected at once became aware of his distinction. His swagger grew more pronounced. He bullied his penmates. He was as conscious of his own superiority as the runtish female was of her disqualifications. The other puppies ganged up on the paragon when his manners became unbearable. During these brief moments of strident combat, she did her part, but when we intervened, she withdrew into a corner and brooded on her own inferiority.

Already, immature whiskers had fuzzed out about her muzzle, granting her face a peculiarly wistful and chubby expression. She was smaller than any of her brothers and sisters and not always meek toward them, but with Althea and me she was eternally hovering on the verge of complete collapse. She was placating, then timid, then abject when we approached her. When we addressed her,

[ 172 ]

she flopped over on her back, round, bare stomach exposed, paws waving apology.

Hers had been the identical breeding and rearing of her rowdy brothers and sisters. These showed us scant respect. She, continually, begged our pardon. Neither inheritance nor environment could explain her nature. As much as any Scotty pup possibly could be, she was the reincarnation of Ben Bolt's dim-witted Alice.

October had dawned when I saw Althea in the pen one morning. She tarried there so long that I left my work to find what was the matter. She held the runt in her arms and looked the other way while she spoke with the brusqueness beneath which shame lurks.

"Maybe it would be better, since we want to be sure we get a good dog, if we kept two pups."

This was heresy and it was uttered by the woman who had protested against the prospect of any more dogs at all. I stared, but Althea would not meet my eyes.

"Don't be foolish," I bade her. "We know perfectly well which is the best of them."

I had the feeling, familiar to all husbands, that beneath the calm surface revolution was gathering. Althea said:

"Yes, of course. But don't you think really that two puppies would be more fun to have than one?"

Mine was the helplessness and indignation of one who finds that his own weapon suddenly is being used against him. I could not speak for a moment. Althea cuddled the runtish puppy. At last, I managed:

"Didn't you say yourself that we didn't need any more dogs; that one pup was all you could possibly endure?"

[ 173 ]

"That," said Althea, brought to bay, "has nothing to do with it. I didn't know this poor little thing then. She needs us. She's sensitive and frightened at the very least thing. I'm going to keep her and that's all there is about it. I don't see, if you can pick a puppy you want to keep, why I can't, too. Do you, Cricket darling?"

"What did you call her?" I asked when speech returned.

"Cricket," said Althea serenely. "It's her name. I named her a little while ago and she's my own dear puppy."

"All right," I said and there was something in my voice that roused Althea to a shamed defense.

"And besides," she went on, with her cheek against the pup's head, "we couldn't possibly give her away. It wouldn't be right. She's so timid and high strung that she wouldn't be happy with strangers and, besides, anyone who took her would be certain that she'd been beaten. You'd say so yourself if you hadn't known her all her life. Do you want your friends to believe that you abuse puppies?"

"Are you trying to make me believe," I asked, "that you're really only thinking of my reputation?"

"Well," said Althea, "not entirely."

"I wondered," I told her. "Have it your own way."

Thereafter, we got rid of our surplus as rapidly as possible. Friends came and received and departed, too enraptured to notice Althea's twitching face as our late dependents left us forever. There remained at last only three, our paragon and the more obvious misfits—Cricket and her crooktailed and cow-hocked brother. Our friends had taken one look at his rear elevation and then had chosen for themselves some other pup among the available.

I still was sure, and all the laws of the stud book supported me, that my choice had been correct. The paragon was good and he knew it. Cricket looked wretched when I spoke of her points but Crooktail did not care. He had a heart above cow hocks and an outrageous terminus. All the optimism his sister should have shared had gone into him. In this best of all possible worlds, he played happily and when his brother and sister wearied of games, he invented others for his own solitary amusement.

He was light of headbone but he had a merry and mildly elfin expression. His almost black eyes—which should have been hazel—looked up with gay confidence upon mankind. Neither doubt nor any hint of apology clouded them. It was a swell world and he was friends with all of it, wherefore he carried his atrocious tail proudly and without a trace of shame. Normally, it resembled a miniature boathook; in moments of excitement, it looked more like a fragment of pretzel, but it was clear that he liked it. He liked everything.

He admired Althea and me and through some odd quirk of his small mind constituted himself our page. When he was unpenned and walked abroad with us, he took the hem of her skirt or a cuff of my trousers in his mouth and strove to bear either in stately fashion. He did not tug or tear. He simply walked, dedicatedly, beside us. The trick pleased Althea, but it gave me a strange and prejudiced gait.

If he esteemed us, the fine distillation of his worship was reserved for Black Boy. He considered the vast dog Nature's crowning achievement. So much of reverence, profound and undiluted, was in that admiration that it embarrassed even a spirit so avid for popularity as the Newfoundland's.

For as long as Black Boy could endure it, the puppy would sit in front of him, a small punctuation following a giant capital letter, and openly adore. He attempted no familiarities. Obviously, he only wished to gaze with flagrant worship upon so superior a creature.

After a little of this, Black Boy would begin to fidget. Veneration so seldom had been accorded him that he did not know how to handle it in allopathic dosages. He would smirk and wall his eyes. One could almost hear him blurt "Aw, shucks!" Later, he would try to pretend the pup was not there. When this failed to alter anything, he would growl. Thereupon, his devotee would abase himself, saying as clearly as prostrate body, flattened ears and quivering tail could speak:

"How vcry truc! How absolutcly sound!"

Praised beyond endurance, Black Boy at last would rise, stalk away and, finding that his adorer followed, snarl and flee.

And then, suddenly, it was the afternoon when the last of our beneficiaries arrived to take away our final spare pup.

They waited in the living room while I went to the

pen to get the offering that, with each step I took, seemed more and more sacrificial. I opened the gate. The paragon popped out and, unbidden, swaggered off to the house. I watched his confident progress. There could be no question about it. He was a very good little dog. I did not see Crooktail in the pen. I called impatiently and felt a responsive tug at my trouser's leg.

He sat at my feet, quaint and eager. The eyes in his triangular, upturned face held a gleam of the worship he reserved in full for Black Boy and in his mouth was the edge of my trouser cuff. Thus we went to the house, he gravely pleased, with his atrocious tail curled over his back; I, crabwise and knowing precisely how Abraham felt when he sharpened the knife to butcher Isaac.

The paragon waited on the porch. He scuttled in when I opened the door. I picked up Crooktail and followed. He snuffed my neck and jammed a cold nose into my ear. I placed him in Althea's lap so that she might bid him farewell. The pup we had chosen to keep strolled about the living room, receiving as his due the acclaim of our visitors. They had had Scotties of their own and knew a good dog when they saw him. One of them said dutifully at last:

"And the other. He's rather nice, too."

Our last spare puppy stood in Althea's lap, his back to the company. His paws were on Althea's shoulder and his head was against her cheek. The awful tail quivered. I glanced again at his self-approving brother and looked at my wife. She said nothing, but she held Crooktail close. I heard myself announce:

"We like him. He's the one we're going to keep."

I picked up the paragon. He nipped me. I told my guests:

"Here's your pup."

And here are ours, end products of Althea's and my attempt to breed a really praiseworthy Scottish terrier. The combined bodily virtues of Wullie and Cricket do not equal those of him whom, in a spasm of emotion, I gave away. We have small pride in the puppies who are our pick of their litter, but much delight. Rapturous letters from four households merely confirm what already we suspected: We parted with all our better dogs.

They will be more credit to their owners than ours ever will be to us. They may win untold yards of blue ribbon and even, conceivably, become champions. We don't care. No other member of the litter accompanies his mistress abroad, decorously, gravely, with the hem of her skirt held in his jaws, or regards all mankind with as happy a trust—a faith so engaging and a face so bright that it enables one to forget the structural defects of his rear end. No other puppy of our breeding needs so sorely our patience and understanding to adjust her crushed spirit to the world of men as does Cricket, the eternally convinced of sin.

Her perpetual state of apology does not carry over into her dealings with others of her own genus. She is technically respectful to Black Boy, Dougal and her mother, but toward Wullie, she displays a sisterly truculence. Together, they supply most of the uproar that this October has produced on our hillside.

Our elder dogs have acquired the sobriety and discipline that life, in time, imposes on all living. They have fitted themselves into existence here. We and they have attained a singular, dovetailed unity. Wullie and Cricket still defy our home's calm routine. They are gay, headlong, perpetually eager. Such creatures are sufficiently rare in the current world to be precious, whatever their points.

Two pups are, as Althea held, more fun than one. We find mirth in our youngsters' identicality of attitude and mood. They sit together, prick-eared, solemn, laughable. They range the fields side by side, like one dark little dog and his shadow, and hunt mice with kindred futile pouncings. There is entertainment in their playful assaults upon each other and more in their frequent brawls.

In moments of violent dispute, they employ a system effectively used yet apparently not invented by the totalitarian nationalities. Combats between Wullie and Cricket produce an amount of horrid noise incredible when one considers the size of its sources. These raucous outbursts smite the inexperienced heart with terror and bring its owner running to avert murder. The rescuer finds two bristling Scottish terriers, knee-deep, not in the Marne but Munich.

Squalling, raving, they stand shoulder to shoulder with whitely rolling eyeballs and gnashing teeth, but their jaws clash on nothing more substantial than atmosphere and, for all their passionate seething, they keep their hideously contorted faces averted. Possibly, they are look-

ing for the appearance of an impressionable old gentleman with an umbrella.

Already, their promotion to permanent posts in our
household has had a regulatory effect on our pick of the
litter though this may be apparent only to our own in-
dulgent eyes. Cricket, it seems to us, cowers less and is
not quite so profuse in her voiceless apologies. Wullie
still stages mental sit-down strikes when his will and
mine cross, but his obedience is improving, though his
tail gets no better.

Neither puppy has acquired any profound reverence
for Althea and me, their only comprehensible deities, and
though, for the welfare of themselves and of our possessions, reformation must come, we shall be a little sorry
when Wullie and Cricket fall into the more decorous cadences to which we humans and the elder dogs march.

Gleeful insurgence born of sheer delight in being alive
is singularly endearing. This is a fact which, if too closely
inspected, leads one to wonder whether the religious do
not worship their deities in the worst possible ways;
whether mortals may not best serve the Giver by taking
shameless joy in the existence He has granted. I doubt
whether God makes a present to any man so that he
may mourn over it and be wretched.

Bryant must have been following the perverse human
doctrine when he moaned in brisk meter over the coming
of the melancholy days. That supposedly dismal period
will be upon Althea and me in a week or so now when,
save for the clattering brown oak leaves and the dark
patriciates of evergreens, woods will be bare and winds,

ranging through them, will speak with a shriller, sharper voice. Frosts will tan our fields and earth and sky will harden. The prospect does not depress us.

We know that, as the outer world grows bleak and hostile, delight draws in and centers on our house. We know that the sparser life of the wintry northland will concentrate about our dwelling. Already, the deer are on the move, out of the forest and into our mowing and pastures.

Our car's headlights find them when we are abroad after nightfall—bright, incredible creatures against the darkness. The fact that, within the last fortnight, I could have hit a dozen deer with a flung apple does little to elevate in my esteem the sport of shooting them. It is hunger and, I hope, a sense of at least partial safety that has pulled them toward us. They have worn a deep path along the charged fence that protects our vegetable garden. Occasionally, some specially well-insulated individual gets through the wire. We shall have fewer brussels sprouts this autumn than we had hoped, but we do not specially grudge them.

Birds are returning, too, to board the winter with us. Hairy and downy woodpeckers and nuthatches call ever more frequently at the suet rack. Jays and chickadees dine regularly at our feeding trays. They will be our intimates for five months now. Transients—myrtle warblers, fox and white-crowned sparrows—visit us and tarry a space and then depart as the compelling summons from the south calls them forward.

[ 181 ]

## The Circling Year

I have revised materially my mental picture of bird migration since I came to live here. I no longer cherish the illusion that the small voyagers fly directly from summer to winter ranges. There is drama to the picture of a bird packing up his belongings in northern Canada and taking the air for a non-stop passage to Panama, but among the feathered creatures I know best I am certain no such spectacular enterprise occurs. Most birds do not journey at express speed. They use a local with many stop overs.

I suspect that it takes the white-crowned sparrow much more time to travel from Ungava to Texas than most persons imagine. I know that those who stop here on their trip are not hurried overnight guests. They dawdle and linger for as much as a week before they pull themselves together and depart, probably to spend an equal amount of time at some other hospitable spot a short way along their route. In spring, they are even more deliberate.

Soon, the last stragglers in the southward flight will have left us. The final obstinate bluebird, the ultimate resolute song sparrow will have gone. Our household, indoors and out, will have made ready for winter, with storm windows in place and fuel tank filled; with wood-shed crammed and a vast heap of kindling under its cap of tarpaulin.

Life already grows more deliberate. We shall find ourselves marching contentedly to its ever slower beat. Cold will lock our land. Acreage will not call us, peremptorily, persuasively, away from our dwelling. We shall live here more serenely, with fewer distractions. We shall read again the gospel that is closed to landless men and know once more the contentment and the strange sense of safety reserved only for those who legally and spiritually are actual parts of earth.

In the calm and quiet time now imminent, frigid mowings, pastures and woodland will be our shield and within their protection, Althea and I shall feel tension slacken and find thoughts no longer crowd and jostle each other, and discover we think more clearly because, actually, we think less.

Men cry that the world plunges toward doom. We look out upon our own small patch of earth and disbelieve. If the tumult disturbs us, we need not hear it. We are not compelled to listen to the radio; we place no special credence in yesterday's newspaper. Dread, which is the direst part of any ordeal, does not stalk us here.

And if the worst should come, the steady voice of our farm tells us our land shall no longer be our pensioner but our partner and, thus united, we will not perish. Fields, even fields as wholly fallow as ours, are a sedative and a reassurance.

It may not be well, since men believe that their gods best are served by lamentation, for Althea and me to be so wholly content. Yet, whatever the future holds, we have had for six years, on our own land, in our own way, tranquil delight. That knowledge cannot be taken from us and the reputedly melancholy days of November will burnish it still brighter.

[ 183 ]

# CHAPTER ELEVEN

# November

IT IS November now and Althea and I can almost sight the end of one more twelve month voyage. It is November and the year draws gravely toward its close. Earth reaches back toward port. She must sail only the small and shrinking segment before still another circle has been made perfect.

Longer shadows stretch northward at noon across the golden grass and each day the sun rises and sets further down our valley. His brilliance is not dimmed. Never is his radiance stronger than now, but he drops toward our packet's weather rail and, blessed more briefly by his presence, earth grows chill.

I feel, when I go abroad, that it is within the world itself that the growing cold abides. The silent days are almost unbearably bright. You squint and flinch when you come out of the house into the sunlight's glare but, where it does not fall, earth turns to iron. Bare soil is cracked apart by small ice wedges that sparkle in the fissures. Where the rowen's rough pelt clothes meadows, stones that lately protruded sink into swollen soil that is thrust upward by waxing, internal cold.

Perceptibly, the rigor advances. Even on the warmest

[ 184 ]

days, shadows are chill. Each morning, our fields retain a little longer than heretofore a dully glittering augury of imminent snow. Each afternoon, when my dogs and I tramp up through the woods to our hilltop, I see new signs of winter's advance. Springs on the pasture slope that advertise themselves only by cow-trampled mire in summer, have fathered miniature spreading glaciers. Ice creeps out from either shore of our little brook and where the dark current is not too swift, already has bridged the flow.

Stillness rules the sunshine. There is frigid, deeper silence in the shade. The considerable tumult wrought by the passage of my dogs and me is our world's only sound and in our forest nothing lives save unkempt yellow blossoms that star witch hazel thickets.

We ramble, my dogs and I, through the annual, uttered forecast of mankind's eventual sure end. Only one of our party pays it any heed and it depresses none of us. We smell the provocative fragrance of leaves. We mark the intricate cobalt mosaic contrived by twigs against a blue sky and from the bald pate of our farm we look down upon our dappled hillside, green and dull maroon, hatched by the white downstrokes that are the bare bodies of the birches.

The air makes breathing something more than an automatic satisfaction. Sweat that the climb and the sun have sponsored is a pleasant, chill tingling when I pause. Since the world now is barren and lifeless, there is keener joy in the mere fact of existence. I find in the yearly prediction of all life's extinction no cause for gloom but, instead, an odd fortifying serenity.

Here with a freezing land about me is great beauty of sky and clashing light and shade; of bright ranges and dusky valleys. These preceded man. When the last of the acrid human ferment has evaporated, they still will endure. The loveliness of earth has a comforting permanence. It is worthy of the clumsy worship I accord it.

I find my mind following unaccustomed ways when I go abroad with Black Boy, Meg, the puppies Wullie and Cricket and sometimes the elderly Dougal on November afternoons. Occasionally I pause and survey my own thoughts and wonder why they do not depress me, since they deal with matters that men forever have swathed heavily in crepe. Consciousness of imminent death is an inevitable yet a not unkindly companion for a countryman who roams his own land on a November afternoon. It goes beside me as I work my way uphill.

Ours is a deliberate progress. I pause to cut away with my belt ax the sinuous, black wild grape that is strangling a tall oak with a Laocoön embrace. I tarry to chop down beech saplings so that the young hard maples among them may have space to grow. Such enterprises have no clearly definite purpose. I am not reserving the oak for profitable timber nor shall I endure until the little maples are mature enough to tap for syrup. My small improvements to my woodland are for its benefit, not my own. In some inane way they are the caresses I give a beloved possession.

Our climb is as aimless as usual, but it is an easier progress than in summer. Sunlight, that comes down strongly now to paint the pale tree trunks, warms without oppressing me. Keen air enlivens an aging body. I find myself treasuring the consciousness of my own vigor and ease of breathing. Surely the time when I no longer can make this stiff ascent is still a long way off.

My dogs accompany me each after his own fashion. Black Boy ranges through the middle distance but every so often comes bounding back, forelegs stiff, ears flopping, tail waving, to assure himself that I am still moving in my awkward bipedal fashion. Meggy has vanished as is her wont. She has a bottle genie's gift for disappearance, particularly unlikely in one so solidly plump of figure. At some time, after we have reached the hilltop, she will materialize as inexplicably as she departed.

The older dogs conduct their enterprises with more purposefulness and self-control than the puppies. Youth's enviable, endearing vigor fills two low black bodies almost unendurably full. It stimulates, it inspires. It cries for immense activity lest the sheer pressure of being alive burst the small containers. The woods before me are filled with a furious sound of scuttling for scuttling's own sweet sake. There is hot galloping up banks. There are avalanches down again in a rattling spray of dead leaves; alarums and excursions, bustle and confusion, hue and cry. The world to Wullie and Cricket is young and very fair and replete with the most distracting allurements, none of which they follow to any clear conclusion.

I look away from their disheveled elation and peer behind me for Dougal. When we crossed the pasture, he had dropped back. There is no sign of him now and he does not appear when I call. Dougal has gone back to the house, not deeming the ascent that so enraptures his juniors worth the effort. He may squire Althea, who takes a more deliberate and easier way to our hilltop. He may, with the weight of his nine years upon him, simply stay at home.

Not the least of this world's disorders is the fact that one cannot progress, stride for stride, through life with the dogs one loves. Nine years ago, the puppy Dougal ran far ahead of us as Wullie and Cricket do now. Thereafter, I overtook him and for a little while he moved beside Althea and me, sharing the enterprises of sober maturity. Now he falls behind. He who recently was so much younger than we is older now. I see him turn away at the outset of one of the walks that used to be his soul's delight and plod back home and the pathos of the small, renunciatory figure smites my heart. Is he aware that he grows aged? I do not know. Men are too prone to read into the lives of their dogs their own most piercing thoughts.

Presently, our oldest dog will die. This is the inevitable anguish we took upon ourselves when first we made Dougal ours. He will die and, in a little space, so shall I, for this November I am well into my fiftieth year. The annual cycle may be no more nearly completed than my own footless and happy life. On this still, autumnal afternoon, I find myself turning the thought over in my mind.

[ 188 ]

It is grave but not frightening. The knowledge that I shall pass the half-century mark in a few more months is not dire. I knew more prospective dread when I stood on the threshold of thirty.

Life is good. I take more sober joy therein than I did twenty years ago, but I have learned since then that men commonly place too high a value on mere existence. Longevity, of itself, is no great benison. Only the superstitious and infatuated hold obstinately fast to a no longer profitable investment. I do not crave excessive length of days.

I am closer now in my life's progress to the aging Dougal than I am to my gleefully scrambling puppies. Actually, I know no more of death than they or he and I dread it—or so I believe—as little. Anguish, mental or physical, is a dreadful thing. I think of death as I climb the last and steepest pitch of my hill and come out of the woods upon the sparse brown grass, the twisted wild apples and the stunted birches that adorn its crest. Mine are not fearful or even uncheerful thoughts. It is strange that men should dread complete immersion in that oblivion wherein each night they dip themselves so willingly.

This may be heathen unenlightenment. I like to believe that it is, rather, the serenity earth grants those who love her passionately. Death comes swiftly, easily to her own most intimate creatures. To be as the beasts that perish is an enviable lot. I find the Hereafters contrived by other men less sustaining. I do not fear in this year's November —and, it may be, my own late autumn—the simple return to earth of the loaned and briefly animated clay. All this I consider soberly but not anxiously as I clamber to our hilltop to meet Althea and Dougal there.

If the day be clear, we tarry on a slope where the sun dwells longest, gloating with a miserly zest that six years' possession only has intensified over the wooded slopes, the brushy pasture and the smoother tan mowings of our farm. Four hundred feet below us and a third of a mile away, shines the white oblong of our home. If from our height, Althea and I see a stranger's car drive up the hill to our dwelling, our delight in our remoteness is intensified. The remaining days when we can loaf abroad together this year are too few and precious to forsake them for mere callers.

Dougal and Black Boy sit close beside us. Meg pops suddenly out of the atmosphere to stand before us with a guileless, if breathless, expression. Wullie and Cricket, who already have journeyed, thanks to their aimless forays, twice as far as any of us, work off a surplus of energy by chasing each other furiously in circles. Their activity punctuates and stresses the cold, clear stillness.

This grows more severe as the sun drops and drives us at last from our height. We rise and go downhill in the midst of a canine rabble, pausing often as the lower light grows richer to revel in the subtle and uncelebrated beauties of a November late afternoon which, in Vermont, fills itself quietly with unlikely associations of red and blue.

I am not sure whether these odd comminglings be due to a peculiar slant of the sunlight or to some unique quality of the air, but Althea and I know that nowhere else in the year do we find like unobtrusive splendor. It is not October's flagrant pomp. Only the reflective eye absorbs it. Like great wines, the colors of sunset time in November cannot be gulped. They must be savored, from the garnet glow that spreads upon the grass, through the misty lilacs, heliotropes and amethysts that hang in the treetops of the nearer slopes to the cerulean hues of the further ranges. These deepen and shift and recombine as the sun goes down. The world at last is gray and there is frost in the air when Althea and I get home. The warmth of our dwelling is comfort to weary bodies, the yellow brilliance of our lights a relief to sated eyes and the smell of cooking from the kitchen is a pleasant promise.

There is work that I deserted in midafternoon still waiting for me. I go upstairs. Meg, a dog of lively imagination, who fancies herself not only a great huntress but, at the moment, my literary inspiration, accompanies me. She curls up on my lounge, sighs loudly and at once is asleep. I sit down at my typewriter with an odd feeling of eagerness, not for my writing, but for what lies beyond the next two hours.

Once, only the prospect of a night of Manhattan revelry would have quickened a like expectant glee. Now, I am looking forward to nothing more gaudy than a quiet meal with Althea in our own home and a calm evening before our hearth. To such a level advancing age and a stultifying rural life have lowered—or raised me.

[ 191 ]

When the tranquil hours have passed and Althea and I have gone to bed, I shall lie in the still, cold darkness and consider contentedly the events of the day, no one of which has been of any moment or interest save to ourselves. Before slumber takes her, Althea may ask:

"Didn't you think that apple pie was good tonight?" Or, "Wasn't Wullie funny today with Black Boy?" Or perhaps, since she is not of those who believe the gods best are served by disparagement of life, "Isn't it beautifully still and aren't we the lucky people?"

We may be the stagnant, the self-centered, the complacent, also, but we are indeed the lucky people as Althea and I judge fortune.

Ours is not the common rule by which most folk measure success. We know that covertly we are pitied by persons more strenuous and more free than we. Theirs may be the clear sight and ours the purblind, for Althea and I are the earth-bound, the groundlings, who have been disparaged by the aspiring and energetic since time's beginning.

We concede this, but we are the peculiarly difficult erring who are too contented in their errors for reform to move them. We even attain further heights or depths of smugness. We actually are sorry for those who are sorry for us.

The forward looking and ambitious who cannot understand our calm happiness are those who in their middle years did not pull out of a groove of existence, come to Vermont and espouse, polyandrously or polygamously, a haggard old farm house and an inordinate amount of scrubby acreage. They have known neither that marriage nor its consequences. Argument with them would be a little like discussing photography with the blind. They simply are not aware what life on your own intimately possessed, ardently loved land can do to you or for you.

That transformation has been for us so gradual, yet so constant, that only occasionally do Althea and I appreciate the changes the last six years have wrought in her and in me, and the alteration our hopes and purposes have sustained.

These latter are humbler than once they were, but they atone for their lack of magnificence by the fact that some of them will be fulfilled and most of them can be if the gods send us sufficient length of days and just a little more cash. None of them threatens the pace of our present existence. We want to live precisely where we are living and very much as we are living for the rest of our lives, with our days moving quietly and our land about us.

Ours is without doubt an egocentric and stodgy existence. Association with our farm has turned most of our values upside down. Or perhaps, after all, it merely has set them at long last properly upright. It is hard to believe affrightedly in the looming of chaos when season follows season in immemorial, reassuring sequence, when ours is the certainty that still other Novembers will cast their bright silence over our hills and fields long after we ourselves have gone.

Wherefore, we find that Stalin and Hitler are annoyances only a little above our need for more rain before the ground freezes tight and considerably less dire than the fact that I cannot find the peaches that, long since, must have become brandy.

Althea takes no part in my search save to spur me to more defiant endeavor by her quiet air of justification. The original project was wholly mine. Its execution, as far as it has gone, has been mine also. Clearly then, my current predicament is—like most of my miseries—my own fault.

One could, I was informed two years ago, make a more than merely palatable peach brandy by filling a crock with alternate layers of peaches and sugar and, thereafter, burying the receptacle deep in earth for two years. Though I purchased the crock and its ingredients, though I supervised the intensely sticky work of preparation and thereafter interred the mixture, I am not yet able to confirm or denounce the reliability of the recipe and the chances that I ever shall grow slighter daily.

I· buried the laden crock behind the woodshed, two years ago last month. The enterprise required a deal of excavation and when it was completed, I smiled at Althea's suggestion that I place a marker over the mound of freshly restored earth.

"What for?" I asked. "You don't think I could forget where I'd done all this work, do you?"

"You might," said Althea in an experienced tone.

"Ridiculous," I told her.

She made no answer, but I have no difficulty in recalling how she looked. I still see that piously patient expression whenever I refer to peach brandy.

"I think," I said to Althea approximately two years

after the interment, "if you'll scald out some demijohns, I'll dig up that crock before the ground freezes harder."

In the light of what has happened, I suspect my confidence seems comic to my wife. To me it appears pathetic. I got pick and shovel and went out back of the woodshed. I stayed there a long time before I even started to dig.

Two years had done much to this more than normally neglected area of our farm. Matted and frost wilted grass covered the precinct. It hid all traces of what once had been an obvious burial mound. The terrain's outline as well as its herbage seemed to have altered. It didn't look at all like the back of our woodshed as I remembered it. Bushes and a couple of locust saplings flourished where none had grown before. I surveyed the prospect and felt inside me the growth of dismay and the singular queasiness familiar, I suppose, to all husbands whose wives are right as often as Althea. I hadn't any clear idea where I had buried the peach laden crock. Nevertheless, for the sake, not only of the putative brandy, but also of my connubial repute, I had to find it.

The crock had been buried toward the woodshed's north end, I was sure—or pretty sure. So I went to work. My pick's second stroke smote an obstacle that investigation proved to be a boulder of considerable dimensions. Most certainly, the brandy did not lie beneath this. I chose another possible site. Doubt mounted, though energy flagged, as I enlarged and deepened the hole. When this had reached a depth at which no one in half his senses would have buried a crock, or even a horse, I gave up. Obviously, my guess had been wrong and by now my emotional confusion was such that I knew it was utterly impossible to make a wiser hazard.

"The demijohns are all ready," Althea called sweetly from the kitchen.

"That's fine," I blurted, "but—well, I'm not quite ready for them yet," and with panicky energy attacked another spot. It seemed a more unlikely site than the first, but I couldn't be sure. I dug until I reached a firm ledge that apparently was part of Vermont's skeleton.

The demijohns, bright, sparkling and empty, were ranged on the sink when I at last entered the kitchen. Althea looked at her loam-clotted, apoplectic helpmeet.

"Find it?" she asked.

"Well no," I told her. "That is, not exactly. The truth of the matter is that I can't give any more time to digging today. I've a lot of important work to do. The peach brandy can wait."

"I see," said Althea slowly.

"I know you do," I answered. "And I know too what you're pleased with yourself for not saying. Probably, it isn't very successful peach brandy, anyway. Maybe it will improve if I leave it where it is a while longer until—"

"Until when?"

"Until," I broke down, "we can afford to hire a steam shovel to dig all the earth away behind the woodshed, for I haven't the least idea, my dear, where I buried that crock. I'm only sure of the fact that I'm not going to mine for it any more."

[ 196 ]

Althea didn't say "I told you so." She couldn't help looking it, but she didn't actually say it, which is one of innumerable reasons why I go on living with her.

It may be that, next summer, I shall drive more exploratory shafts into the already riddled precinct behind the woodshed. My search is over for this year. Frost daily drives deeper now to make digging ever more difficult and I have inherited other, more pressing outdoor enterprises. Frederick, our hired man, has left us for the winter and until next spring mine will be the duty of attending the vicissitudes of a perpetually semimutinous water pump, burning the day's vast accumulation of waste paper and incinerating the garbage. These two last tasks already have made me wish that ours was a wholly illiterate household that lived exclusively on sandwiches. Frederick would be gratified if he knew how much I miss him.

I might have begged him to tarry longer and postpone my servitude had I not known that such a plea would have been vain for the deer season cometh, when no Vermonter worthy of the name can work and still retain his face in the community.

For ten days, the herd of semidomesticated and exquisite creatures whose presence in any landscape doubles its beauty will be assailed with varying degrees of skill and a wide assortment of lethal weapons from sunrise till sunset. For ten days now, Althea and I will flinch at each gunshot and try, most unsuccessfully, not to think of what the report may portend. For ten days we shall live in a wretched, half-nightmare.

## The Circling Year

The zest with which otherwise civilized men turn to slaughter is bad enough, but it is not shame for our own species that is the most nearly insupportable trial of the deer season. Fifty years' residence with mankind is sufficient time to make most illusions concerning it drop away. Nothing can be done, by treaty or by gospel, to diminish human blood lust that esteems the killing of even the mild and the wholly defenseless "sport."

We have stopped worrying over the innate and ineradicable savagery of man which he shares with no other living thing save the weasel and which, in time, must utterly damn his race. We still shrink from the sight of deer carcasses tied to the running board of a car—the slender limbs no longer passionately fleet; the dreary, antlered heads, once so proudly alive. We walk hastily, too, past the open air shambles on Brattleboro's Main Street, where scales straddle bloody sawdust and triumphant hunters bring their kills for weighing. These are part of the deer season's ordeal, yet not its sorest. Vermont, that exhaustively examines each citizen's abilities before he is permitted to drive a car, makes no inquiry as to a man's skill with firearms before issuing him a hunting license. Thanks to that purblindness; thanks also to the willingness of many hunters to shoot first and look afterward, if at all, the woods and the valleys of the brooks to which parched and maimed creatures crawl fill, during November's last ten days, with anguish beside which clean, quick death is a little thing.

I do not think it is sentimentalism that makes Althea conscious of agony in the air and quickens in her responsive suffering. I know it is not mere intuition that weights both my spirit and my stomach while the deer season endures, for I have sought through growing dusk to find and end a fawn whose forelegs had been bullet-shattered by some inferior to the suffering beast and I have heard Ray Pratt tell, in the dry voice beneath which our game warden hides pain, of the mercy killings he makes as the deer season's aftermath.

Perhaps my morality is lamentably warped, yet I hold that he who cripples and leaves to exquisitely slow death a live thing has wrought unenviable iniquity. I know that each hunting season does more incalculable harm to man than to the defenseless thing he slaughters.

My own generally not too stalwart belief in an incandescent and sulphurous hell is fortified each deer season. Lacking it, how can lovers of justice and mercy hope for the requital of those who annually cripple beautiful, terrifically vital beings and leave them light-heartedly to protracted torture?

It is well, I think, that Althea and I were obliged to buy with our home so much apparently unnecessary land. Our acres are not only our beloved possessions and our insulation against the woes of the world. They are my protection, too, for they spread so far that even my loudest comments upon deer hunters cannot reach my neighbors' ears. Probably, also, they shield me from my neighbors' even more justly uttered opinions of me and my own iniquities. It is a good thing in many ways to live on land of your own.

Althea and I hold fast to that pristine certainty. The days of anguish and death are at hand, but beyond them waits winter's quiet, cold and tranquil time. We look forward to it as one anticipates reunion with a cherished friend.

# CHAPTER TWELVE

# December

SNOW FELL lightly just in time to keep the tradition of a white Vermont Christmas inviolate for Althea and me. Our five earlier Yuletides here were more spectacularly supplied with drifted roads and burdened firs and fields smothered in soft brilliance, but Althea and I have been grateful for this mild storm. We knew it was coming for, the day before it fell, the eastern horizon at sunset time was crowned with blue haze and the hills about us wore an inky hue.

All virtue, as Confucius established, is based upon a due observance of the ceremonies. There are a few recurrences in existence too importantly dear to us for variation of their hallowed ritual. This Christmas has been, as nearly as we could contrive, the exact duplicate of its five predecessors.

Long before the coming of the actual holiday, the spirits that transform it, the small, hallowed importances that adorn it, move into our home and our hearts so unobtrusively that we are not actually aware of their advent until, suddenly, we rouse and grow aware that they possess us all.

No one can establish the formula of Christmas. No

one can set forth an accurate recipe for the assembling and combining of its infinite ingredients. Some of these are clearly labeled. There are pages of Luke and Charles Dickens, childhood memories and racial recollections, staves of carols and the scent of evergreens, hearth smoke and tinsel balls and the glow of mistletoe and holly. There are components that men can identify. There are further and obscure essences, spices, flavorings that resist analysis, yet, blending, fill the day with radiance.

Christmas is near when Althea and I begin to display toward each other furtiveness and secrecy that, at any other season, would be downright suspicious; when we leap up and bar doors against each other's intrusion and forestall inspection of hitherto innocent cupboards with frantic cries of "Hey, you mustn't look in there!"

Christmas is nearer still when our son comes home from college and our unwillingness to dim an already perceptible and warming light keeps us from even referring to his last term's scholastic record. The Yuletide is almost upon us when we make two and three and sometimes four trips daily into Brattleboro and come home, overladen, to discover that there still are things we meant to get and didn't.

This year, as in every year, despite long and intense preparation, Christmas Eve arrived with many of our purposes unfulfilled, with sundry plans for the holiday incomplete. Waxing elation let us ignore these failures. We never have been able to celebrate the Yuletide as lavishly as we had intended.

The snow, of which we almost had despaired, lay

upon our mowings and when my son and I went to the woodshed at dusk to bring in the mighty log destined for our hearth on this night of nights, we saw entangled in our dooryard hemlock a star, surely almost as bright as that which hung above a stable.

I remember that, as we wrestled with the Yule log in the bitter dusk we laughed a good deal for no clear reason. Neither of us, I suspect, was as young as, at that moment, he felt.

Superimposed memories of Christmases we already had spent in our own home made this, our sixth, still fairer. It was as though the flavor of old festivity, lingering here, intensified the new; as though an old and dear melody sang in our ears once more with small, distinguishing improvisations.

Again we had rejected more stately spruces and had found at last a balsam tree to occupy an ordained corner of our living room and, conforming to the established ritual, my son and I set it up on the ancient standard, which was an enterprise demanding infinite resource and sagacity as well as a good deal of mutual recrimination. Again, we trimmed its branches, each of us after his own fashion to the accompaniment of much hearty disparagement of the other's efforts.

For a sixth time, we hung wreaths in the windows and upon the doors and balanced on the mantelpiece the rickety miniature sleigh, the Santa Claus and his eight battered papier mache reindeer.

Once more, we established the Crêche in its traditional bookcase alcove. Once more, my mother, after the usual

[ 203 ]

doubts whether she possibly could get away from New York at the appointed time, arrived, incredibly bundle laden, to spend her twentieth Yuletide with Althea and me.

Thereafter, the festival moved its fair and ordained course. Neighbors came on Christmas Eve to make wassail with us and there was good talk and much merriment before the fire in our balsam scented living room where the shadow of the imminent Day erased the lines of caste that normally lie between native Vermonters and immigrants.

Long after our guests had departed and we had hung the time-honored and widowed stockings we preserve from year to year for that sole purpose, Althea and I labored, finding the presents we had hidden and distributing them for the morrow and endlessly imploring each other for heaven's sake to remember where we had concealed this or that gift.

At last, I lay abed and held fast to consciousness for a little while, solely that I might savor the peace that dwelt in the cold stillness and feel the mounting toward its climax of the Christmas insanity. This is dementia that, for its duration, makes you believe the affairs of earth are not as they distressingly are, but as they should be. The delusion waited beside me while I slept and gripped me afresh when I woke.

We opened our gifts in the presence of the entire company, including expectant dogs, whose normal excitement when any parcel is being unwrapped was slightly curdled now by the fact that each of them wore, attached to his or her collar, a large red rosette in honor of the holiday. The radio sang carols for us and through the music and the crackling of paper and the exclamations of rapture, it seemed to me that there came from afar, yet clearly, the jovial laughter of the Founder of Christmas himself.

All day long, I heard snatches of that merriment, while my son and my dogs and I tramped the snowy hills together, while we listened in early twilight to more carols, while friends gathered with us for dinner and while, thereafter, we attended the party Hap Mason, a Yankee of Yankees, gives every Christmas night for the folk of an entire region.

Here, under the spell of the Day's blithe madness, men who ignore each other during the rest of the year meet as brethren and through the tumult of their greetings, I heard again the gay, enduring mirth that, if audible too long, might wholly overturn and reorder a world.

It seemed to me then; it still seems to me now, while the year wanes and the echoes of one more vanished Yuletide still sound in my ears, that the thoughtless ordinary of earth with an odd, sure instinct accord to Christ by their celebration of his nativity delights that actually were close to his heart—gifts, merriment, pleasant food, good wine and their sharing with friends. At Christmas time, we make over our dwellings with feasting and revelry into havens where the Author of the holiday himself might feel most nearly at home. It is strange, if he were actually the saddened aesthete creeds have made him, that his anniversary by most ancient tradition always has been merry.

Paul, the strict organizer, and Paul's successors have bleached and wilted their Deity, making him sorrowful, destiny-enslaved. Multitudes do not follow the dismally dedicated, nor are men eager to have him at their festivals as an honored guest. Fragmentary and amended scriptures still picture him as an outdoor man who knew and loved the ways of birds and beasts and flowers; an ardent hiker, a good fisherman, a keen sailor. He liked parties and dinners and picnics and he was popular with publicans and peasants and even certain rich men. Children, too, were fond of him. His immortal laughter once again has made our Christmas the crowning holiday of the circling year.

That year now is almost spent but the Christmas snow still spreads its transforming fabric over our world. Wind and sun have thinned it to a powder on our mowings and pasture, but in the woods it lies more uniformly, pale background for the involved patterns of tree trunks and branches, a revealing garment that discloses each hollow and ridge of our land. Shadows dwelling on the snowy ground stress contours that at all other seasons are hidden. Flakes, lying most deeply in neglected ruts, revive dim pathways and woodroads, long unused. These ghosts of old ways that haunt our timber recall themselves to us each December, like Christmas cards from half-forgotten acquaintances.

The last few days of the year go by in grave beauty that early twilights quicken into splendor. The sun at setting now sends its radiance from far to southward, so that hilltops take new shape in the singular ruddy light and shadows stretch at unlikely angles across the valleys.

In this, the year's last homeward reach, when my dogs and I come in from our tramp in the late afternoon, I find myself delaying return to my work upstairs. Instead of climbing to face my typewriter again, I linger at a living-room window while the sunlight fades from the ridges and the clear yellow western sky takes the greenish hue that foretells a colder morrow.

This vigil has grown into a rite during the years I have lived here. I cannot wholly describe its purpose. It is mystical, superstitious, sentimental. Late December's days become weighted with inordinate value. I watch their passage regretfully.

The aftermath of cold still prickles on my face and stings my ears. My body knows the ease that is violent effort's blessing. About the living room where shadows gather, the dogs sprawl in the enviable, utter relaxation of their race. Even the puppies are content to rest for a little after the up and down miles we have traveled.

It is time to turn on the lamps and light the Christmas tree again, but I do not stir. Instead, I wait by the window to watch the night move in. Another year has almost ended. It is well for one who has been so much its debtor to attend its passing. The twelve month voyage is nearly over. Watching the winter night creep up the valley, I list haphazardly the profits it has brought to Althea and me.

These are not wholly calculable and are, in general, unnegotiable. Most of what we have won since the argosy stood out to sea, only a day more than a year ago, is peculiar treasure, infinitely precious to its owners yet of no possible use or interest to aliens. Most folk would disregard, few would understand the contents of the corded bales we have brought back, Althea and I, from our annual venture.

Part of men's incomprehension would rise from our inability to fix with words the virtues of that cargo. Furthermore, the current world has come to disregard the matters that we, in the time of our dwelling here, have learned most highly to esteem. Even to the eyes of our friends, our cruise to the twelve ports of the year has won us only humble, perhaps even shabby, gains. I am heartened a little by the belief that He, whose birthday we have celebrated, would esteem them as Althea and I do.

Our latest voyage has altered us. Matching our current life and its purposes against our existence six years ago, even I am a little startled to see how much we have changed. Men may hold that we have slipped backward. It may be so.

I know that the direction and the focus of our ambition has been radically adjusted. The pace of our life has grown steadily slower. We find delight centering more and more upon what, to us, were once elemental and disregarded matters. We have lived more closely to earth than to men and we have become, perhaps, not only racial dissenters but actual heretics, adhering to a heathen creed that I have found heartening and stabilizing—a creed that has abiding hunger for the fairnesses of earth as its principal tenet and a keen delight in little things as its only ceremony. It is a simple faith but a sufficing. The rewards it offers are immediate, not pledged to our account with some dim hereafter.

Our bodies and spirits have become tuned to the simplicities of quiet living in the abiding calm of rural Vermont. We have learned that contentment, even joy itself are not pegged to any fixed social standard. Neither luxury nor pomp is a necessary ingredient of delight. It can be found, clear and intense, by folk who live like Althea and me, in the mere state of being alive.

This I truly believe, though I find my current ambitions and indulgences forever more of a bewilderment to my onetime intimates, yet a constantly growing satisfaction to myself.

How can I explain that I get more sustenance and elation from a tramp such as I have taken this afternoon with four disreputable dogs up an ice-locked brook, along an ancient road that stubbornly preserves its integrity though all its bridges have rotted away, past a towering hemlock grove and through pasture to my own hilltop, than two hours spent at any theater in the world could afford me? How can I make the uninitiated understand that in the even flow of life here, small events spread wider circles than epic happenings which fall into the torrent of urban experience?

I have created nothing; I have bettered no one but myself and a Newfoundland and three Scottish terriers by my wintry rambling. It is entirely possible that mine is a selfish and unaspiring way of life. So it may be, but men who reach ambitiously for the stars ignore much loveliness spread at their feet and sometimes come to the end of their quest more empty-handed than I.

The substance and flavor of any joy cannot be relished completely unless there be time for its savoring. There is time here. It intensifies senses that haste and anxiety only blur. Thus, matters of living that seem routine to the urban and sophisticated are events of stature to me.

He who speaks with fifty men in a day has less sense of intimate companionship than I who may in that time hold deliberate Vermont speech with only a single visitor. He, in departing, leaves behind an impress of himself, clear, unmarred.

The meal at the day's end once was only part of an accustomed routine. It is now an event flavored by hunger, spiced by consciousness of the long, quiet evening beyond.

The drink one gulps as a gesture of conviviality has only the end effect of wine that is shared with a friend. Haste ignores the scent, the flavor, the subtle aftertaste.

Few urban folk ever learn the great delight of weariness, which is not the taut fatigue of overwrought brain and nerves but a blessed sense of emptiness, of dreamy ease that only spent muscles can bestow.

Such things are the sharper pleasures of my life. Beneath them, constant, unobtrusive, is a sense of communion with the earth itself. This is something that the city-bound never know. It can lift and fortify other men than Antaeus.

# December

All Vermont is fair. Unlike most states, it is universally lovely save for an occasional mill town along its rim where the disease of industrial squalor has begun and halted. Eastern Vermont is the fairer portion. All who dwell here say so anyway. Our farm, as Althea will tell you unless I hold her silent, is the fairest precinct of all. So, at least, it seems to her—and to me.

About us wherever we look is beauty, constant, assuaging, delicately reflecting the weather's whims and the changing seasons. Our eyes absorb it in all our waking hours and by that continual association it seems that part of it lodges within us, so that eventually we become in some odd way associates of the loveliness that laps us, companions to the experiences and vicissitudes of our own land.

We blend and merge, home owners and their home, so that the spiritual boundary line between mortals and less animate acreage grows increasingly hard to maintain. The years we have spent here have clothed all our land with reminiscence, with the comradely memory of shared experiences. Each rod of our farm, each contour, almost every tree speak to us with a provocative kindred voice.

I hear this wordless, sustaining speech as I stand at the window and watch the night come gravely up the valley and consider the year that moves toward its ending. It will be most memorable to other men for savage and dire matters. These have shaken Althea and me, yet I think that in the future we shall recall this twelve-month that is passing, not chiefly for the horror it has harbored, but as the cycle in which we had our attic insulated and our house repainted, as the birth year of Meggy's puppies and the time of Dougal's death.

I can see his grave from where I stand. I hacked down through the frozen soil and buried the body of our senior dog where in life he delighted to sit, just beyond the garden wall, to watch the valley with a grave and contemplative air. He was a dour yet unfailingly courteous person, the only thorough gentleman our house has permanently harbored since we came to live here.

When incurable suffering smote him, we granted him that final, thrice-blessed mercy of painless, unending slumber that men perversely withhold from their own stricken kind. He had had nine years of free and happy life, which is as much as animals of even my own breed can hope from existence.

So Althea and I tell each other, yet I still find myself, when I reward my dogs, taking from the closet five biscuits instead of four and when dinner is ended and cigarettes are lighted, my hand still gropes to find the wet nose, the tough shaggy body that tobacco's scent once unfailingly brought to stand beside my chair. The ragged hole in the turf where he lies will heal more swiftly than the emptiness he has left in our lives.

Above the icy gleam of West River, blue dusk is fading into gray. About the feeding tray and suet rack, downy and hairy woodpeckers, nuthatches, irreverent chickadees and bullying jays flash and pause and circle, completing the supper that fortifies them for incredible slumber in leafless, zero woods. We shall have more boarders this winter than ever before. The thought is warm about my

heart. The increasing tameness of our pensioners cheers
me.

Bluejays who, when we first came, fled like the guilty
sinners they are at the least sound or movement within
the house, now regard me with bright, irreverent eyes
when I peer through a window pane within two feet of
their rascally persons. The shy hairy woodpeckers merely
hitch half way around the dangling suet bag if I come
out and stand beneath it.

These matters we rate among our chief accomplishments for the year, but the trust that the chickadees have
learned to place in us is our dearest treasure. This winter,
after much lingering at arms' length and protracted and
doubtless unflattering comment upon my presence, they
have so far admitted me into their confidence and fellowship that they take sunflower seeds from my palm or
perch upon a doughnut, while I hold it, and hammer
away at its fat brown crust.

The day when the hero or idiot of their jaunty, black-
capped race first hopped down from a twig upon my
hand, pecked at a knuckle to see if I were edible and
then fell to work upon the doughnut I offered will stay
bright in my memory while my mind endures. One of
us, perhaps both of us, had the awed feeling that a treaty
that had lain defiled since Eden's fall at last had been
restored. I have not yet won the chickadees' complete confidence. They still display in approaching me the dubious advances, the swift recoils of instinctive abhorrence.
They feel as I do when I force myself to pick up even

the most harmless snake and the chickadees have far more warrant for their revulsion than I for mine.

A flock of plump, dark birds come through the evening sky and settle in our drive. The pine grosbeaks who have called twice before to fill their crops with sand spread on the slippery way have returned again. Their presence so early in the winter indicates cruel weather further north.

Watching them peck and kick the gravel about, I add a further item to the debt of gratitude I owe the town authorities, who not only made our hill safe for passage on Christmas Eve, who not only indirectly brought the grosbeaks here but who also taught me another lesson in Vermont strategy. Now that I have learned it, I need never fear that my road will be too glassy for safe passage.

It was treacherously iced all the week before Christmas. We slid down and skittered up to the accompaniment of anguished gasps from Althea, who, as the holiday neared, grew ever more insistent that I lift my voice in the loud squawks that most effectively pierce official ears in this region and demand that the drive be sanded.

"Listen," I bade her, "if I begin to yell in mid-December, you know what'll happen. By February, when we really need it, everyone will have grown so accustomed to my noise that I won't get sand then."

"Have it your own way," Althea answered, "but I don't see how the neighbors we've asked in for Christmas Eve are going to get up this hill as it is now."

"That's their headache," I said. "I do it every day."

We need not have disputed. The problem was settled for us early on the morning of December 24th. The heart-warming Yuletide spirit may have been partly responsible. Now that the bright insanity has passed, I suspect that the sanding of our road was due more to the fact that several of our prospective guests for Christmas Eve were town officials with high respect for their own necks. One of these telephoned Althea early on the morning of the twenty-fourth.

"How's your road?"

"Slippery," Althea reported, "but we're using it."

"Been sanded, hasn't it?"

"No."

A pause followed during which Althea could feel that her questioner deplored the fact that she was being so unhelpful.

"Don't you," he asked and his voice was reproachful, "want we should sand it?"

"Why, I don't know," Althea told him cruelly. "We get up and down it all right."

"Well," the desperate man blurted, "I'm going to have Harold Reed bring over a truckload right away and do a good job on it. That's not a safe road if it isn't sanded well."

Toward midmorning, another authority and imminent guest got me on the telephone.

"I been thinking," said he. "You ought to have sand on that road of yours. My truck's on the way up now with a load of it."

"It's just been sanded," I told him.

"Oh," he said. "Bob beat me to it, eh? Well, I'll tell you what I'll do: I'll pile my sand alongside the road and then if it should get slippery again before night, you can spread it, eh?"

More sand, I think, came onto our road this last Christmas Eve than it has received during all our previous winters. Hereafter we need dread neither ice nor sleet in planning a party, just so long as we include a selectman or a road commissioner among the invited guests.

The evening star is burning in the sunset's ashes and, responsive to its light, trimmed Christmas trees in the dooryards of the little town down the valley suddenly are small clusters of colors. I watch them and wonder how, with so great a weight of literary tradition against them, New Englanders have dared to retain their love of Yuletide splendor. Yankees are hard bitten and profoundly distrustful of pomp and ceremony. *The Scarlet Letter* proclaims it and so does *Desire Under the Elms* and most intervening New England novels and plays. Yet, six times here in Vermont, we have seen the joy and the hues and the festivities of Christmas immerse and transform a whole region.

Towns are brilliant with garlanded lamp posts and festoons of electric bulbs. No church, however small, lacks a Christmas pageant. Each schoolhouse is visited by some unhappy male who has been dragooned into appearing as Santa Claus in cotton wool and scarlet calico before a delighted if not wholly credulous audience. Baskets of provender appear miraculously on the doorsteps of the underprivileged and on Christmas Eve the young people of our town pile into Harold Reed's truck and embark upon the hazardous ordeal of singing carols through the length and breadth of the community.

This is an enterprise fraught with some peril of frostbite and much more of acute indigestion. The face of each householder at whose dwelling the truckload pauses for song would be blackened if he did not summon the singers in for refreshment. As midnight nears, we hear the truck snort up our drive to the last stop of the pilgrimage. The engine dies. There is giggling, a false start or so and then throats, hoarsened by at least twenty-five previous repetitions, lift for the last time, "It Came Upon a Midnight Clear" and follow that with "Silent Night." Thereafter, Althea calls from our doorway:

"That was lovely. Won't you all come in?"

She blows her nose and I know why. It has been lovely to hear and see in the starry winter stillness and, if the music has not been perfect, we have no warrant for believing that the first carolers followed any earthly system of harmonics.

They troop in, two dozen boys and girls whose cold faces are even more vivid than their snow suits. The shy decorum that grips Vermonters of any age in an unfamiliar place possesses their spirits, but their appetites remain undaunted. Chief of the Yuletide marvels in our town is that even youngsters can absorb the heterogeneous provender the carolers are offered during their tour— doughnuts, cookies, pie, popcorn, apples, cider, milk, coffee, peanuts, maple sugar, cake, candy, sandwiches— and still have any digestive systems, let alone hunger, remaining; yet there was only one backslider in this year's truckload.

He was a small boy with an expression of anguish nobly borne who sought, on entering, a chair in the living room's far corner and sat there during the entire visit in the swollen and apathetic attitude of an ailing chipmunk. He did not utter his woe in specific terms, but his face was eloquent and the single syllable he spoke was freighted with distress.

Each time edibles were offered him, he squirmed, wrapped his arms more tightly about his midriff and delivered his sole articulate comment:

"No," he moaned and turned his head away. "No, no, no."

I grin remembering him and, still considering the brilliant nebulae that are the lighted Christmas trees in our valley's gloom, recall that during the Yuletide of a year ago, I portrayed Santa Claus for the children of the West Dummerston grade school. It was not one of my more successful impersonations. It may be that my native ineptitude prevented a renewal of the invitation this year.

I recall, in this connection, the tale told in hollow tones of a person of my acquaintance by his justifiably aggrieved wife. It appears, as she relates it, that her husband was bidden to exemplify the good Saint Nicholas for the school-attending youngsters of his neighborhood.

The night of his performance was chill, but it was not the temperature alone that made his feet cold and, before his spouse disguised him, he fortified his craven spirit and physical person for the role.

As a matter of fact, his wife informs me, he went in for fortification with the enthusiastic energy of a whole regiment of engineers and when he saw in a mirror the wreck his well-meaning spouse had made of his normally not too alluring self, he fortified himself further to forget the horrid sight.

Beneath the flimsy scarlet tunic, cruel attention had been called to his figure's weakest point by the none too successful application of a pillow which gave his abdomen an oddly rectangular inflation. Even when he scowled, his visage was affrontingly merry, thanks to eyebrows and whiskers of cotton his wife had pasted on with spirit gum, and nose and cheeks smeared to a bibulous hue with lipstick. It was not, his helpmeet insists, entirely the material disguise that made him seem alcoholic.

This long-suffering woman accompanied Santa Claus to the school, first supplying him with a string of sleigh-bells that were to furnish offstage noise. She reminded him that he was to approach the building with a good deal of jingling when, and only when, the signal light above the door had been turned off. Then she left him in the night-immersed car to his own thoughts, which she trusted would be sobering, and a bottle for which she had forgotten to search him before they had left their home.

It was a long wait. As a matter of fact it was materially longer than anyone connected with the affair had expected. At last, the good saint was roused from revery by a viciously hissing voice close to his ear. It demanded:

"Do you realize, by any chance, that they've been turning that light on and off for the last five minutes?"

The rest of the tale is considerably garbled and depends upon which of the couple you choose to believe. It is alleged that Santa as he approached the school employed the sleighbell string as a skipping rope. This is denied, though the wretched man admits that, in the course of his advance, he did trip over something.

It is further charged by his still outraged helpmeet that his gait as he approached the Christmas tree was definitely unsaintly, that his attempts to register Yuletide cheer resulted in nothing more praiseworthy than an abhorrent leer and that he misread most of the labels on the presents.

I do not deny that the impersonator's appearance was made even more regrettable by the loss of one eyebrow that sweat, inspired by the heat of the room and the abdominal pillow, melted from its moorings. I concede the eccentricity of his manner but hold it was caused chiefly by a growing awareness that at any moment his beard was due to fall from his perspiring jowls, and Althea can persist in her wrong thinking to the end of time without convincing me that I really cried on departing from the shambles, "Cherry Mistmas to all!"

I still feel it was through oversight rather than by design that I was not asked to be Santa Claus again this year.

I turn on the lights in the empty living room before I go upstairs. Tomorrow will mark the year's end. Our now quiet dwelling will harbor many of the friends

whom reputedly hostile Vermont has given us in precious
abundance during the last six years.

They are the chief and perhaps the only considerable
treasure I list in my haphazard inventory. The remainder
is composed of comparatively little things. If there be no
other great triumphs on the roster, there are few dis-
heartenments.

It is an oddly reversed sieve in which the gains of our
year have lodged, so contrived that most dull importances
have slipped through and only dear insignificances have
been retained. More strenuously ambitious folk may decry
the substance of our annual trove. I wonder whether the
final tale of my existence will prove them so.

For, if quiet joy be the measure of a life's success, then
mine already has been abundantly justified. Each year
that Althea and my home and I dwell in intimacy re-
iterates the reassuring doctrine that the simple way is
neither ordeal nor boredom. It has, I whisper to myself
as I go upstairs, the calm surety of the circling year itself,
that bears most kindly those whose lives are surrendered
to its course.

Before I light the desk lamp in my attic workroom, I
peer out through the dormer window. Frost already has
begun its nightly etching on the lower panes, hiding the
eloquent land that is wholly Althea's and mine. Looking
upward through the still unclouded glass, I see only dark
sky and belted Orion climbing in the east and the shine
of other stars—the light-houses, buoys and markers on the
course our argosy will sail when it stands out on the

morrow's midnight, bound for June and back again to still another December.

On that ordained great circle, there still is promise of small adventure for us. There is the certainty of reunions, fairer still, in the twelve ports along the orbit of our passage. Out of the sense of completion that has been mine at this, a year's end, new eagerness is growing.

By deepening snow and waxing cold, by earlier dawns and perceptible seconds added to each pale sunset Althea and I shall know that the new, year-long voyage begins and that again we shall be humble shareholders in its enterprise.